HOLLINGSWORTH

HOLLINGS*W*ORD PUBLICATIONS
PHILADELPHIA, PENNSYLVANIA

Not Another Tear: Moving from Pain to Purpose
Copyright © 2018 by Sharon Hollingsworth

All Rights Reserved ® Printed in the United States of America. No part of this book may be used, stored in a retrieval system, or reproduced in any manner whatsoever without prior written permission except in the case of brief quotations embodied in critical articles and reviews. For information contact HollingsWord Publications at www.HollingsWord.com.

Library of Congress Cataloging-in-Publication Data
(LCCN): 2017901615

ISBN: 978-0-99822751-1
EBook ISBN: 978-0-9982275-4-2

LCCN Imprint Name: HollingsWord Publications, Philadelphia, Pennsylvania

Hollingsworth

"Not Another Tear: Moving from Pain to Purpose"/ Sharon Hollingsworth
p. cm.

1. Spoken Word Poetry/Narrative 2. Women and Trauma 3. Self-Empowerment 4. Performance Poetry 5. Overcoming Personal Traumas 6. Original Dramatic Poetry.

This book is printed on acid-free paper.
Printed in the United States of America
Book Cover & Interior Design by Exodus Design Studio

10 9 8 7 6 5 4 3 2 1

First Edition

DISCLAIMER AND LIMIT OF LIABILITY
Although anyone may find this book of poetry and narrative inspirational, this book is sold with the intention to only inspire and entertain readers, and should not be used to take the place of expert certified counseling services on any topic or advice written herein.

If you are experiencing emotional, psychological, spiritual, relationship, or family challenges, please consult with a qualified professional specializing in your area of need.

All Products by Hollingsworth

Not Another Tear: Moving from Pain to Purpose (Series)
- (Book) Narrative and spoken-word poetry
- (Book) Original empowerment quotes and affirmations
- (Journal) Blank writing journal

Not Another Tear: Moving from Pain to Purpose
(CD and Digital) Spoken-word poetry performed by Hollingsworth and featured vocalists.

Victims of Circumstances: Where Pain and Possibilities Are Colorblind (Novel) Part one of a two-part series
Available 2019

The Dream Series (A Six-Part Personal Empowerment Project)
1. What Are They Calling You?
2. Seed Planters
3. A Born Conqueror
4. Toxic Connections: People, Places, Things & Thoughts
5. Live Now!
6. Dear Destiny

For products and services information, to place an order, or to join the author's VIP Mailing List, please visit
www.HollingsWord.com

DEDICATION

Dedicated to those of us who stayed far too long immersed in our pain, past traumatic experiences, insecurities, bad relationships, and failures, all the while taking care of others and neglecting ourselves.

Somewhere along the way, we forgot our own strength, value, purpose, and beauty. Here's to finding them all again and rediscovering ourselves after the pain.

—SPECIAL DEDICATION—

For every dream denied; for every tear you cried; for every struggle you endured; for every headache and heartbreak; for every promise broken; for every moment you felt inferior, discouraged, or underappreciated; for every teachable lesson you gave; for every time you stood up for me in the presence of my bullies; for every moment you sacrificed to raise me as your own child until your last breath; and for *never* saying to me, even in your deepest anger, that you "wished I was never born," I humbly and gladly dedicate this project to you, my grandmother, (the late Minnie Ree Hollingsworth).

Where you lacked in patience and resources, you made up for it with love, and by serving as an example of *'How to make a way out of no way.'* Thank you. (RIP)

ACKNOWLEDGEMENTS

To Kristine Cotterman at Exodus Design Studios, I love the book cover and interior layout! Thank you for your expertise and professionalism. To the three keys of my heart, K, T, W. You know who you are. I love you always. In all of your endeavors, I wish you massive success, joy, and peace in abundance.

To the God of another chance who keeps on blessing this imperfect being…thank you for never giving up on me.

"Life has its own brand of pain but if you can power your way and grow through it, and not allow pain to stop you, you are most certainly guaranteed to win. Therefore, never stop pressing forward. You are far too important for you to give up on."

~ Hollingsworth

CONTENTS

At the Beginning of My Tears — 1
    At the Beginning of My Tears — 2
    Hostage — 10
    I Remember — 13
    Vision — 18
    Highly Misunderstood — 20
    Drafted — 23
    DNA = Donor Never Around — 26
    Scarlet Red — 31
    Sistah2Sister — 33
    Forgiven — 34
    Face of Stone — 36
    Precious Moments — 37
    I've Lived the Life — 40

Ashamed — 43
    I Wish I Could Tell Her — 44
    Stranger in My Bed — 47
    Letter to Mr. Abracadabra — 49
    It Happened in the Bathroom — 51
    I Stayed Far Too Long — 53
    It Isn't About Me — 56
    Because She Yearned — 58
    Ashamed — 61
    Unnecessary Struggle — 62
    Good Morning, God — 63
    Never, Never, Never — 64

This Thing We Call Love — 67
    Plastic — 68
    I Am Home — 69
    Gone Are the Days of the Young Girl with Blues — 71
    Boys Who Chase the Wind — 72
    Poison — 73
    Trapped in Between Loving and Longing — 74
    I'm Sorry — 76
    When Love is Plagiarized — 77
    When Nightmares Becomes Real — 78
    This Thing We Call Love — 79
    Alone — 81
    I Want a Man — 83

...And More of *This Thing We Call Love* — 87
    Uncontrollable — 88
    Tsunami Love — 91
    One of The Greatest Rhythms God Has Ever Made — 92
    Children Are People, Too — 94
    I Never Thought — 96
    Rebirth — 97
    Confessions — 99
    What Defines a Man — 102
    Distant Lover — 105
    Catching Eyes — 109
    Rhythm of My Pace — 112
    He Was Born into This Rhythm — 113
    Baddddd! — 117

The Allures of Darkness — 121
    Standing at the Edge of Midnight — 122
    The Allures of Darkness — 123

They Call…But I Don't Answer	125
They Call…But He Doesn't Answer, Either	128
On the Verge	131
Emotionless	132
Vicious	133
Voices in Her Head	134
Dark Rage	136
Just Wondering	138
White	140
The Quiet Aching of Innocence	142
Dismissed	145
Sometimes I wonder	146

On the Shoulders We Stand Upon — 149

Today	150
Flame	153
On the Shoulders We Stand Upon	155
Carrying to Term	159
Dear God	160
Love	162
The Satisfaction of Labor	163
When Agony Becomes Certain	164
Healing Must Be Demanded	165

I Cry No More — 167

I Cry No More	168
When You Speak My Name	172
Hometown Girl: Aiken, South Carolina	177
Simply Beautiful	181
Oh, Bully, Please!	182
Still Standing	183
Shine	185

Sleep Sweetly	186
Inside	188
Swim Lessons	189
Keep Dancing	190
A Special Tribute to Ms. Diane Patterson	191
"Give Pause"	192

Word from the Author	194
Bonus Exercise	195
How to move from your pain and into your purpose	

About the Author	205
Book Description	207

At the Beginning of My Tears

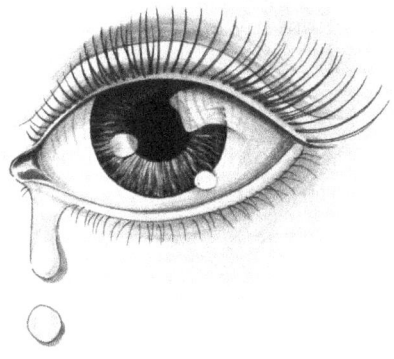

At the Beginning of My Tears

Like an invasion, abrupt images from the past catapulted through my mind. Suddenly, I found myself being thrust without warning back into a history that I had once drunk heavily to forget. And after no longer using alcohol as a crutch, I tucked away the past—deep like a buried treasure—only to now have it reemerge with a vengeance. Hyperventilating, I clutched my increasingly heavy heart as I began to sob uncontrollably before my knees buckled. *Bam!* My body gave way and hit the floor like a sinking stone. I was suddenly that terrified thirteen-year-old girl again, chased and then subdued by the five familiar strangers. I could still hear the splash of water that hit the floor when they grabbed my arm. I could hear the slamming of doors and the sounds of my desperate screams that went unheard.

At age twenty-five, I could still feel the aggressive touch of their vile hands that threw and held me down and fondled my young, undeveloped breasts and vagina. I relived the moment when my breath was snatched away by those same suffocating hands that covered my nose and mouth in efforts to silence my cries. I could smell the stench of every violating act that was forced upon me. I relived the moment when it became clear that even though I could point out the predators, justice never came for me—or for my twelve-year-old friend, who was fortunate to break away from the clutches of one of them and ran to get help. Onto another flickering moment: I could hear the rage in my mother's voice as she repeatedly expressed her regret of my being born. I could see the drunken evilness in her eyes when she attacked me with her violence and the ugliness of me returning blow for blow after growing tired of being treated as her personal punching bag.

Once again, I was that frightened thirteen-year-old girl who was stuck standing in the doorway, watching my grandmother vomit violently into a bucket after the chemotherapy treatments, while her mother (my great-grandmother) lifted up her weakened head to steady her. I could still smell the lingering odor of her vomit and could hear and see her helplessly gag, repeatedly. I could see my grandmother, the woman who raised me, suffer in agony as she withered away. Then, I could see myself standing in the doorway, watching her in fear and great sadness. I was unable to speak, unable to move, and unable to breathe.

Further, I relived my poverty—not that it had ended at the time, but it was of greater severity back then—at a time when there was no food to eat and no water to drink or to bathe in. When there were no lights to see with and no heat to keep warm. I relived eight years of being bullied from elementary school to middle school and being the lonely, awkward little girl who played alone and ate her lunch alone. I relived the haunting moment of realizing that I had become yet another statistic by being both a high school dropout and a single teen parent. I selfishly and ignorantly passed on that daunting legacy to my daughter, who, like me, has no father.

I relived feeling the impact of the two-by-four that struck aggressively across my temple when I was yet thirteen years old, the protruding knot that grew out of the side of my head, and the ten years of pounding migraines that followed. I relived how I hated my uncle Jimmy for that and how I still hated him at the time for deliberately swinging that piece of wood in a drunken rage—giving no thought to the value of my life. I relived the moment of squatting secretly for hours behind some bushes, waiting for him to emerge as he returned home, contemplating my sweet revenge of striking him from behind with the wooden baseball bat I had in tow. I wanted him to feel the agony of being violently and intentionally struck in the head. I relived the moment when I relented after seeing him unknowingly walk past me and how my sudden rage turned into sorrow.

I became angry with myself that I couldn't pull it off. I hated that I loved him enough to do him no harm but that he had failed to return those sentiments to me. I relived the moment when the police were called and how justice was never served or sought after once he had run off. I also relived that invaluable moment when I realized the importance of never becoming what you hate. I relived the moment when I was fourteen. My uncle's wife pounced on my 110-pound frame, knocking the wind out of me, prior to punching me in my face and other parts of my body. Intoxicated and in his underwear, my uncle rushed into the bedroom and pulled his wife off me.

This act of violence erupted as a result of their three children fabricating a story that I had punched the youngest child in the chest (who was about four at the time). They were all under age nine and already had the ability to plot lies in retaliation for not getting what they wanted, which was quite disturbing. And what they wanted was to stay up all night. I had been forced to babysit them earlier that evening when my uncle and his wife had gone out to the local nightclub. The kids had all been put to bed by their mother. However, approximately five minutes after their parents had left, all three simultaneously leaped out of bed and ran into the living room where I was sitting. They began screaming before blasting the radio and dancing in the middle of the floor. The oldest shouted, "It's time to *party*!" That was around 10:00 p.m.

Admittedly, I stood up and yelled to the top of my lungs, "Oh hell no! Get back in that bed right now, or I'm telling!" One licked his tongue at me and another rolled her eyes, as they all reluctantly proceeded back to their bedroom. I never touched either of them, but that wasn't the story they told to their parents. For dramatic effect, the four-year-old even held his chest, and expressed feeling pain. Shortly after being assaulted, I found myself running down the street to the police station after 2:00am in the morning—bare feet, wearing a busted lip and a bloody nose (coupled with scratches and other bruises). Beaten up over lies!

I relived the moment when justice once again eluded me because the police did nothing after speaking to the adults. My uncle and his wife informed the officers that I was homeless, and they graciously took me in when no one else in the family would. My bruises were the result of my aunt "chastising" me after I physically assaulted their "helpless four-year-old child." I was a child without a home and without a voice. I relived the agonizing hurt that came from feeling unbelieved, undervalued, and unloved. I felt powerless to do anything about it.

I relived the moment when my grandmother's body was lowered into the ground and how I numbed myself to prevent feeling the loss. I didn't cry during the funeral. I relived the moment when the realization of my suddenly becoming orphaned hit me like a ton of bricks. In my family, we had always lived our lives at the bottom, and until my grandmother's death (which created a domino effect of the unraveling of everything), we had been fooling ourselves, perhaps, into believing that the only place from the bottom was up. However, with this loss, life unveiled another bottom by kicking the one out from under us that we were accustomed to lying on. It sent us on a freefall toward an even deeper bottom. This bottom came without remorse or warning. It didn't care that we were already dysfunctional, poor, impoverished, and broken. I therefore learned at an early age that even the *bottom has bottoms*, and suddenly, I found myself forced to relive what that felt like.

I relived the moment when I paced back and forth in the middle of Kershaw Street in Aiken, South Carolina, alone, in the pitch blackness of night, playing Russian roulette with my life. I was angrily screaming at God while hoping a speeding car would come and put me out of my secret misery. I had had enough! I relived the moments of being lied on and being lied to. I relived my own failures in relationships, school, and in life. Hit with numerous unrelenting and unstoppable flashing moments, I became overwhelmed. I didn't know where the pain stopped and where the real me, truly began. I was the epitome of the pain I bore.

However, I smiled on the outside so that no one would notice my pain because frankly, I didn't think anyone gave a damn. The one person who I knew for certain cared about me had exhausted her last breath due to the cancer that had ravaged her body. I relived my loneliness, my regrets, my destitution, my homelessness, my heartbreaks, my failures, my fears, my insecurities, and the vacant feeling within when *love* had left me. There, on my dining room floor at age twenty-five—and all in one afternoon—I found myself weeping twenty-five years' worth of sorrow. Like a levee, something enormous inside of me had suddenly broken, and the fragments and the severity of my brokenness were scattered about and had become exposed.

Even alone, I found myself weeping in shame for carrying all of this now-exposed baggage for all of those years. Immersed under a flood of assorted emotions, I thought I was losing my mind because up until that point, I had faked happiness and wholeness. I had faked having it all together for so long after burying the past. I had convinced myself, as I had others, of this falsehood—of this notion that I was whole. In reality, I was nothing more than fragmented pieces of a poisonous past, layered with traumas, fears, insecurities, self-hatred, and doubt. I was not the definition of my true, authentic self but rather the definition of all of the circumstances I had endured over the years. I was like a hologram—only appearing to be living in the physical presence—when in reality, my heart, mind, and soul were trapped in history.

There I was, thinking that I was in control of my past because I had tucked it away—only to realize that up until that moment, my past still had control of me. With haste, I found myself trying to regain my composure, so I hurriedly wiped away my tears and proceeded to get up. Sobbing, I walked down my long hallway toward my living room before abruptly stopping at the threshold that divided the hallway and living room. I could see my daughter still sleeping soundly on the living room couch. I was relieved. The last thing I needed was for her to witness the emotional unraveling of her mother. I began to force myself to take slower and steadier deep breaths while wiping away tears that continued to fall.

By this time, my eyes were puffy and red; I couldn't breathe out of my nose. It had sprung an uncontrollable leak, just as my eyes had done. To add to this, I couldn't stop my body from trembling. Needless to say, I was a complete mess. However, a voice (that I know was the voice of God) whispered to me and said, "You cannot outrun the past. It is time to face it." I resisted at first, only to decide moments later to surrender. I returned to my dining room, still weeping; my chest felt incredibly heavy. Nevertheless, there was something about this voice that gave me an inner peace and comfort that surpassed all of my understanding. It made me realize that my heart, soul, and mind were being renewed and were undergoing a seriously long-overdue deep spring cleaning. For many years, I had been caught somewhere in between history and destiny, and up until this point, history had been winning.

It became abundantly clear that what I had thought I needed to be free from my painful past wasn't what I had needed at all. I had thought I needed to get justice and to have others right their wrongs...to have others apologize...to explain...to show up for me. To validate me. In reality, with the help of God, I only needed to give *myself* the permission to heal and be courageous enough to face my hurt and then...to let it go. I realized that one's willingness to be emotionally healed should never be contingent upon other people. Justice may never come. People may never be sorry, and even if they are, the answer as to *why* they hurt you will *never* justify the hurt. It will never suffice. It won't make you feel better. And for years I wanted to know *why* my mother and my father didn't show up for me. I wanted to know *why* my grandmother had to die. I wanted to know *why* I went through what I went through, only to discover right there in my dining room that the *why* was irrelevant.

Furthermore, God had already validated me at the moment of my conception, and behind *that* validation is a *period*. I'm important because I exist. There is nothing a person can do to validate what has already been God approved. With this unfolding revelation, I continued to weep my pain that was being washed away by my tears. Every tear had a purpose—a clear, divine assignment. With each one, I gave myself the permission to let go of the hurt and resentment associated with every agonizing image of the past. I wept until there was no more weeping to be done…until the images stopped. By the time I had regained my composure, the feelings of heaviness were being lifted off of my chest and shoulders. I instinctively knew in that moment that my life would never be the same. I was now standing on the right side of my history and knew that my path to personal healing was clear. Finally, my destiny was now on the winning end, and my past was being stripped of any further permission to have charge over my life!

Though this was not the day I completely stopped hurting, this was the day I faced my hurt. It was also the day that I made the deliberate decision to no longer allow my hurt to win. It was restoration day one! From that experience, I wrote what has become my personal anthem, "I Cry No More," which you'll find in this collection of spoken-word poetry. Though many are, not all poems herein are reflective of my own personal experiences. Some are reflective of my perspective, while yet others are reflective of situations I've witnessed throughout various periods in my life.

I hope you'll enjoy!

Hostage

Hostage is what I feel!
Trapped inside these four walls against my will,
With no means of escaping out of this reoccurring act of
Raping...

Hostage is what I feel!

When I feel your hands ascending up the curve of my
Thigh and hear the sounds of zippers zipping down, I cry.

Because hostage is what I feel!

When you covered my mouth to silence my cries,
And he covered my eyes to lessen his shame,
When they spread my legs and held them open
To give you opportunity to do what you intended to do
To me...

Hostage.
Hostage!
I say, hostage is what I feel!

When your hands began stroking my virgin clit as
You pressed your inhumane body against mine and
Began to enter that ugly beast inside,

Hostage,
Hostage!
I say hostage is what I feel!

HOLLINGSWORTH

But you didn't get my good friend Kia.

She ripped from your grip
And fled on foot and ran home to her mother
And someone called the police; she knew something
Bad was happening to me.

Although my fear and humiliation were long-lasting,
My virginity was spared by the siren I heard thereafter.
And though you stripped and ripped as you invaded me,
Rescue in uniform came and aided me
Just in the nick of time.

Woo! It just *blows* my mind.

Hostage was I, but for a while
Hostage...I am no longer!

Hostage are you!
Wrapped up in your gated and shackled evil
Minds...appearing to have been human flesh once upon a
Time.

Only wearing cloaks of death that stink up your own
Souls...getting your *kicks* off trespassing young bodies...
You're cold.

Hostage!
Hostage is what you are because of the
Sickness of your own diseased and
Demonic minds.

Hostage is what you are because of the
Humanity that fled from your rotting souls inside.
Hostage you should feel!
Because hostage *you* are!

Hostage...*I am no longer*!

I Remember

I remember the days
When we had no running water.
You remember...the times when we
Had to carry jugs and buckets up and down the street
In our hollowed hands with our bare feet beating
Intensely against the gravel and the Southern sand.
There was no room for young pride.

No, pride had to be pushed aside so we all could survive
As we walked from our house to yours and to yours again.

I remember the days
When the stench of the toilets suffocated the air.
You remember...the only happy creatures there
Were the overly aggressive, buzzing flies
That made their way inside through the broken screen
Door.

I remember the days
When we had no electricity or heat.
You remember...the dangling pots and pans we
Carried in our impoverished hands
To cook and carry our dinner in
From our house to yours...and to yours again.

I remember the days
When we couldn't see or keep warm.
You remember...when we wrapped ourselves in old,
Smelly blankets and multiple clothes to adorn ourselves
In, as the bottom of our feet and toes were frozen—they

Were as cold as ice on the cement floor.
Even with socks and shoes on, we still didn't manage to
Keep warm. Although freezing, we survived the night...
And another and another and another, as we had grown
Accustomed to this kind of plight.

I remember the days
When the only things left that filled the cabinets were a
Near emptied bag of flour, a cup of rice, and a can of
Sardines.

You remember...hanging on to your last bit of pride, as
You worryingly made your way inside of Haron's Grocer,
Pleading for more store credit, secretly hoping and
Praying you'd get it again, so we wouldn't starve to death,
Knowing that we couldn't survive on what we had left.

So from our house to Haron's store and to Haron's store
Again, we carried fifty, a hundred, and sometimes only
Ten dollars' worth of food to feed our roaring bellies.

I remember the days
When we got beatings...the kind that are now classified
As abuse. You remember...when you beat us with
Multiple tree limbs that we were forced to go outside and
Handpick ourselves.

All tied together with a piece of torn cloth, it put the fear
Of God in our bones and the imprint of your wrath on our
Butts and thighs. Years later, when I think about it now,
I still get tears in my eyes.

But…I also remember
That even in our great poverty and dysfunction, there
Was a real sense of belonging to family…you remember
Too, now, don't you?

We were a chaotic bunch but a bunch no less.
The outbursts of laughter that permeated the air as we
Mostly laughed at ourselves were contagious.

We had *some* good times, and sometimes when I find
Myself in solace, I reminisce about those days because in
Some strange ways, they made me the woman that I am.
In spite of our circumstances, there was an untold,
Underappreciated, and unforeseen richness that once
Dwelled within this chaotic bunch we call family.

And *this* is perhaps *why* I sometimes find myself smiling
Through the tears as I think about those years and about
The women who *somehow* held it *all* together.

In spite of the "dys" that plagued their "function," they
Functioned nevertheless: *Richard-Dean Hightower, Minnie
Ree Hollingsworth*, and *Pauline and Corrine Hightower*…all
Gone but not forgotten, which is why I write this!

Oh, how I wish life would have given you more!
More time, more love, more resources, more confidence,
More peace, more hope, more joy…and more of
Everything you felt you had less of!

But now…now that you're gone, the baton has been
Passed, and we've taken it:

Blazing small trails like graduating from high school—
Something you didn't achieve—or earning a college
Degree—something you couldn't perceive—
Far surpassing where you all stopped...chasing dreams
And living our purpose!

*Was this your quiet hope for us underneath that tough,
Exterior surface?*

Yeah, it's true...we had a whole lot of poverty and little of
Everything else, but we had each other. Now it's time that
We act like a family again and be there more for one
Another...again.

Together...let's transcend above the generational
Barriers. The past alone is far too impotent to carry us
To greatness.

And...and we don't have to carry the past on our
Shoulders, the pearls they left behind in spite of and
Because of the struggles...and faith in ourselves and in
God will hold us. Let him remold us.

Because with him, no poverty or struggle is too massive,
And no pain is too broad to overcome.

We can walk with boldness, birthing dreams and blazing
Trails, and surpass where we came from!

And remember, as I too remember, because they are
Watching, and our children are watching...*just* as we
Once were.

Let's make them proud! Let's make ourselves proud, as We remember...*together*.

Vision

Sometimes when I close my eyes
I can still see her in my vision
And can hear her thunderous cries.

She's searching relentlessly...carelessly.

By day
She searches for bread and water and for
Acceptance and friendship.

By night
She searches for a home filled
With love and tolerance.

By day
She smiles a *beautiful* smile
And speaks as though without a care
Blinding *everyone* to her secret despair.

But as surely as the sun rises and sits
Her pain is always there.

So it is by night
She searches for peace and for parental praise.

But neither does she find, for her parents
Have long since fallen asleep and rest
Far below in the earth beneath.
By night

She searches for parties and for sexual highs,
Hoping they'll numb her pain
And bring solace to her cries.

And although she practices this nightly
Until the break of dawn,
Neither is strong enough
To give her what she *longs* for.

By night
She lies in her own vomit in a drunken state.
Men climb on top of her
And enter between her gates.
Without consent or consideration,
Her body…they take.

With her head spinning out of control,
It's hard to determine *real* from *fake*.
So it was by day—the darkest day of all
From the pit of her belly she released
A morbid call
As she…

Mumbled,
Cried,
And
Screamed

For God to take her away
From *this* tormented scene
And so it was…
By night.

Highly Misunderstood

She walks past the *boys* and the GROWN men, too.
Impressed by their masculine eyes that strategically
Follow her hips and thighs as they move HARD
From side to side.

That girl is highly misunderstood—
Looking for love in all the wrong places,
Trying hard to fill the void of Daddy's missing face.

Easily *impressed* by the *whistles* and *stares*,
Whistling is for DOGS, but *she* doesn't even KNOW
To care.

Easily impressed!
That girl is often highly misunderstood.

For they see her as being *easy*—they'd lay with her
If they could...and, oh...do they!

Without realizing that they too are being *easy*—
Thinking not with their *big and brilliant* minds
But with their *small* pecks of "wood" in comparison.

That girl is highly misunderstood—
Looking for love in all the wrong places
Trying hard to fill the void of Daddy's missing face.

Yes!
Attention is what she seeks, and she'll get it

ANY WAY she can—yearning for someone to
Genuinely love her; she doesn't *really* want to be
Sexed by a man.

But with her misguided *cravings* and *their* lustful
Ravings they partake of the *forbidden* fruit,
And when they're finished doing the "do,"
They both come up empty and *still* incomplete—
Never filling up on that "thang" they seek.

That girl is highly misunderstood—
Looking for love in all the wrong places
Trying hard to fill the void of Daddy's missing face

SOMEBODY ought to tell them that
This "sex thang" AIN'T no "love thang"—for they
Don't even compare!

So GIRLchild and BOYchild
Please be astutely aware.

You are worthy of so, so much more.
Do you hear me, child?

Fall in love with yourself, and while you're at it,
Fall in love with God!

He already loves you and knows your yearnings
And your cravings—even before they are *known*
In your heart.

I'm telling you, turn your emptiness *over* to a

Healing, loving, and *all*-fulfilling God!
It ain't hard.

'Cause he did it for me, and he can do the same for you!
'Cause this "sex thang" AIN'T no "love thang,"
For they don't even compare.

So, my GIRLchild, stop being wild!
BOYchild, stop being vile!
You can do so much better.

I love you, but more importantly
God loves you, too.

My GIRLchild...and BOYchild.

Drafted

No scent of your cologne
No pictures of your faces
Only *blurred* memories
That time will soon erase.

No more hellos or good-byes, and
No more looking into your dark brown eyes.

Never *really* knowing your hopes or dreams
Or how you'd hope to one day finish this scene
Called life.

Never becoming men or meeting your future wives,
Seventeen and nineteen years old you both were—
Riding down the highway—oblivious to the fact that a
Drunk driver was about to make you *his* prey.

SOMEONE made a *decision* to drink AND drive
Without giving much thought or care about taking
Others' lives—or *even* his own you see—because the
Predator behind the wheel struck and hit a tree
And was also killed.

Maybe I was wrong to feel...but I was happy he
Didn't Live.

For *all* I could think about were Nathaniel and Dale
And how their bodies were ejected from the motorcycle
Seventy-five feet high and *fell* upon the ground!

Force so *powerful*—blood DRAINED from their BRAINS
And *even* their SHOES had to be found! Breath no more—
INSIDES *shattered* to the core! DOA—dead on arrival.

Not *even* a small glimmer of hope for survival
Out of this *drunken* madness! *Three* families left to
Mourn in *unspeakable* sadness!

Young men of DESTINY
Struck down by DOOM,
PREMATURELY rotting away
In OLD MEN'S tombs!

How DARE he make a choice for them—that they
Would not live! Having the power to *decide* is not just
A RIGHT but a PRIVILEGE and a RESPONSIBILITY that
GOD gives!

But sadly enough, according to statistics, thousands of
People each year are DRAFTED in this army without
Their armor on because ain't no American highway
Is where a battlefield belongs!

But yet here in America *each* and *every* day
The war of drunk driving still rages on...
Making us all prey...*do you hear what I say?*

Statistics ask the question:
What is the financial cost for drunk-driving incidents?
But who can count up the cost for such a loss?

There ain't no cost for a soul

Or for the countless *dreams, schemes, inventions,* and
Stories that never got a chance to unfold.

So if drinking and driving applies to you
Here are a few words I would like to leave with
You, too:

HOW—MANY—*THOUSANDS*—MORE
Have to be STRUCK DOWN and MURDERED
Before you make up in your mind
To get YOUR act together?

Don't drink and drive!

It isn't hard to perceive
So please don't wait until YOU'VE murdered...
Before YOU believe.

DON'T—DRINK—*AND*—DRIVE!

DNA = Donor Never Around

In secret, I wondered: If I truly
carried inside of me, your DNA,
and if so, *why wasn't that
enough to make you stay?*

I found myself reflecting
back on my youth—staring down
dark gutter-filled pathways
to assess the truth,
and to finally slay the dragon
that attempted to set my
destiny ablaze—in lieu of your
absence...

...*long* before I ever
knew that life had dragons,
and that many little girls like me
had no daddy—and long before
I *ever* knew—I had the capacity...
to dream.

Reminiscing on a time
when I coddled wet kisses
and warm beer bottles to cope—
when I clung onto false confessions
of adoring love with naïveté and hope.

That *'make believe'* made me believe
in the lies that the grown men and
young boys spoke.

They played on my insecurities
as a fatherless child—like a
hand-me-down toy.
To them my pain didn't matter,
nor did my void.

Pressured into giving myself away—
weakened by ultimatums and,
"If you love me you will do it"—
those calculated advances, and:
"Baby you know I love you, right?"

All under the dark pressures of dim lit
moonlight...*where my sky and stars had*
already fallen

For a while I played the game
they wanted me to play
because as a young girl with blues—
left, bullied, and *bruised*—
it was a logical step, that the next
would be getting used.

Giving into their lust
in exchange for misguided trust—
so they could combust—
I thought this was the
only way to make them stay,
but just like you, Mr. DNA...
they *never* did.

So, I learned to silence my voice and to
keep my aches and screams inside—
hiding them behind a nonchalant attitude
and a multitude of phony smiles.

For a while as a child, I told people
that my last name was Miles—not
because I didn't like *Hollingsworth*
—my name given since birth.

I chose Miles because that was said
to be *your* last name.

In spite of the obvious rejection,
as a young girl I still yearned for a
father-daughter connection.

Therefore, I created one by the
unofficial taking of your last name,
so I could at least *pretend* I was
claimed—but clearly, I wasn't.
For, all you saw was baggage.

Reflecting back when I was
Six-years-old and seeing you
for the very first time:

You introduced yourself as
my father but not once did
you *bother* to reach down to
touch me—every little girl wants
to know her daddy's touch

But you looked upon me
like one would a dirty penny
found in an alley, rather than
seeing me as your number one.

You gave my grandmother
a measly twenty-dollars.
I guess you thought that was
the total *sum* of my value, and
all of the work my grandmother
had done—to raise me and to
keep me alive.

You left and never returned.
You disregarded me and then
discarded me—your off-spring—
like the wrapper from the
condom you clearly didn't wear.

Was it too damn much to care?

I was severely broken,
but then, so was your manhood
because you failed to do
what a *real* man would
like…take care of
what he has created.

You see, I was *your* production—
Created by a flop—
Donor Never Around!
You're just another deadbeat—
a *clown* without jokes.

Bound to biology, I placed
my value in your leaving
but after assessing the
truth, I've realized that my value
was never tied to you.

For I'm the daughter of the most high
G O D—Giver of *my* Destiny!
He has healed my scars.

I may have been your
inconvenience but I was
His full intention—
long before I was ever
pushed out into *this*...dimension.

Least I forget to mention
I'm not a mere "bastard child"
I AM DESTINY'S DAUGHTER.

#DestinysDaughter
#IAmGodsChild
#MyLifeHasValue

Scarlet Red

Yesterday I bled.
I bled profusely,
As teardrops of scarlet red
Ejected from my vein like pouring rain,
As overwhelming sensations of past humiliation
And pain traveled back to my conscience.

Every waking moment without reason,
You left lesions on my soul
By the persecution of your tongue.
My reputation you murdered and hung.

And like a monstrous, evil vampire, you thirsted
For my blood as you dragged my innocent name
Through the mud.

Like iron brass your fist did become
As they angrily flung toward me.
Why did you abhor me?

I did nothing to earn your animosity,
So why did you commit such an atrocity
Against your own flesh and blood?
Did anyone ever teach you about love?

Contempt did my heart hold as I wished for
Your demise.

You became less than nothing in my darkened,

Swollen eyes.
Like an animal in a cage, my heart was filled
With rage—contemplating your end was all I
Thought of back then.

If I dared to break free from that mental haze,
You would be a distant memory, fading away.

But thanks be unto God for my deliverance
And for all my burdens he helped me to bear.

He is why I've been set free and why you still
Breathe this air.

Sistah2Sister

When I look at you
I see past your vanilla skin
And your beautiful deep-blue eyes.
I don't *merely* see a white woman...
An automatic enemy of my blackness
I simply see...a woman.

No stereotypes!
No racial hypes!

Just...you.
Another beautiful rendition of
God's creative wisdom—
A divine masterpiece,
Created out of the intellect
Of supernatural brilliance—
A *profound loveliness*

JUST AS I AM!

JUST...AS WE *ALL* ARE!

Forgiven

For my abandonment—
You're forgiven.

For all the lies you told—
For the dark future
You forced me to behold—
You're forgiven.

For the nights of terror
You chased me in the summer sand—
For the night you ripped open the can
To cut me...you're forgiven.

For conceiving me without care—
For leaving my grandmother
With the responsibility to bear—
You're forgiven.

For never being known—
For, now I am grown—
And for forcing me to be a kid
Out on my own—
You're forgiven.

But forgiveness does not equate
With allowing you a seat at my table
Because until this day you remain unchanged,
Addicted, hateful, and unstable.

I have spent quite some time
Fervently searching the
Depth, width, and breadth
Of my heart, soul, and mind
Because the last thing I want to be
Is confined to a hurtful past
For you see, my pain did not last.

Hiding behind a trail of psychological and
Emotional contusions, I was under the painful
Impression that I needed you to validate me,
Only to realize that this was yet another illusion.

But as far as I can tell, I wish you well
Because you truly are…forgiven.

Face of Stone

Passerby beckon unto me...
"Smile child and stop looking so E...vil."

    How does one equate pain and worry with evil?

The worry upon my face is that of an *old* woman...
A s*easoned* woman,
A woman with years

    Of experience and struggles behind her,
    With far fewer days left ahead—

    Yet...I am *only* fourteen.

For I am not my own.
Beaten down mentally and emotionally,
I wear this face of stone.

Precious Moments

We shared so many moments in time.
Precious memories of you and I are
Ingrained in my heart and mind:

As children, we played tag, double-dutch, and
Hopscotch outside, underneath the clear blue sky.

Our elders received visits from
Friends and family, both near and from afar
For the Fourth of July: They were *standing by*,
Gazing at fireworks that lit up the sky.

Then, there were those family reunions and
Holy communions when we'd pray.

We would laugh and gossip while sitting on the porch,
Drinking your mother's homemade lemonade
And eating the cake the neighbor baked,

While being serenaded by songs that played,
As we all sang along to the music from that old
Stereo. *Where did the time go?*

We watched our loved ones dance
With red cups in their hands,
But as time went on—
When you went your way
And I went mine,
I thought we would have a lifetime

To get back and to do it all again
With family and those old friends,
But *sometimes* life won't let it *happen*.

Oh, how I miss those precious moments in time,

When we all had one another—
Never thought they would die!
But, oh, the moments shared between you and I
Will last a lifetime.

So I am left to cherish these
Precious moments in our history
When we laughed, prayed, and cried
And wiped each other's eyes—
When we watched our babies be born, and
When we mourned.

Oh, how I miss those precious moments in time

As long as we are alive,
We can make new memories
And add to that great history—
When we share with those precious
Loved ones still here.

Let's hold them dear!

And pass it on to the next generation
Of bright stars, both near and far
Because one day, when the dust settles,
And the stars of now cease to shine again—

For we all will someday be transitioning,
You will be happy and glad that you had
These precious moments in time.

Oh, how I miss those precious moments in time...those

Mothers, Fathers, Grand and Great-Grandparents,
Uncles, Aunties, Brothers and Sisters, Cousins, In-Laws
And Friends, from generations' past—

When we all had one another—
Never thought they would die—
But, oh, the precious moments shared
Between you and I will live on in our
Hearts and minds, and will last a lifetime.

I've Lived the Life

I've lived the life
I've lived the life
I've lived the life

Hanging out in the club
13 to 16 shaking my 'thang'
On the dance floor,
And grinding

Drinking my Bull—
I thought I was cool—
Even dropped out of high school

I've lived the life
I've lived the life
I've lived the life

I wasn't thinking
About the life I lived
And those who died in the struggle
To be educated.

No, I was too damn busy acting
crazy—and at barely seventeen—
I was having a baby.

I've lived the life
I've lived the life
I've lived the life

But one night while sleeping
I had a dream—no, more like
A revelation—it appeared to me

I was falling fast in a deep dark hole.
Death and destruction was the goal.
But then I looked out and saw the light,
And called on the name of Jesus—
That's when He snatched me out
In mid plight

I've lived the life
I've lived the life
I've lived the life

Homeless and hopeless
With no one to care for me
Thought it was how my life
Was meant to be.

I felt betrayed by life,
But God said, *"Child*
This isn't your destiny."

I've lived the life
Lived the life
Lived the life

Ashamed

I Wish I Could Tell Her

The little girl of yesterday...
I can't seem to connect the dots.
Who she was back then,
Today I am not.

Sometimes I wish
I could travel back in time
To embrace her with her first hug,
To ease her worried mind.

I would tell her:
Awake! Awake to your true authentic being!
You are purpose and passion—a whisper from God—his
Love Child.

You are water, air, and fire; you are spirit and flesh
And a giver of life!

There is nothing you can't master—no height you can't
Climb. No dream you can't behold—no matter what
You've been told! You are woman!

Pull back your blinders and all of the layers of
Traumatic experiences that have you caged.
You are not what you've been through.
This is just a passing stage.

Take the bricks that were thrown at you and build!
Build your self-esteem! Build your imagined dreams!

Build!
I would tell her to be bold by daring to dream and to
Take strategic and deliberate aim at the life she so
Desperately wanted.

I would tell her to try harder and to play life smarter.
I would tell her to stop feeling sorry for herself and to
Shake off the worry she felt.

I would tell her to *slow* down and to cease trying
To hurry through life in an attempt to outrun her
Circumstances.

I would tell her to take the chance and dance
More with life but only to a different melody—
One that would propel her to be
The best version of herself possible.

I would tell her
That one day her pain would become her poems,
But pain would no longer be her norm.

I would tell her to lift her head,
And wipe her teary eyes,
And let her know that, without a doubt,
God was standing at her side.

I would tell her to *love* herself
From the crown of her head to
The bottom of her wide, flat feet
With the understanding that God
Made her unique...and that even her

Imperfections are perfected.
I would tell her that her troubles
Would not last always and to
Keep on smiling, living, learning, surviving
And to *never*...stop dreaming!

Stranger in My Bed

In the deep, dark recesses of my mind,
I seek it out…I seek to unravel what makes it tick
And what makes its soul dance
And what drives it to move mountains
And what makes it self-destruct.

In the deep, dark recesses of my mind,
I question *every* conceivable thing about it,
Yet I know nothing at all.

I seek purposefully and relentlessly to develop a
Relationship with it, but it doesn't answer my call.

In the deep, dark recesses of my mind,
I worry, for if I should fail to establish intimacy
With it, it is likely to die and wither away and
Become insignificant and vain, though that's not
My aim.

In the deep, dark recesses of my mind,
I lay in wait…
Hoping,
Searching,
Yearning,
Longing,
Wondering…

Why it's so hell-bent on escaping from my grasp
Though I never really stopped and took the time

To ask.
But to know it to its very depth is to know why I *breathe*.
To know it is to know why I rise out of my bed each
Morning—to know it is to know the very essence of
Who I am!

I want...no! I need
Someone—anyone
To help me find it

Lest it withers away like a falling leaf in mid-October

A
N
D

DIES!

Desperately seeking...
...*Stranger in my bed.*

Letter to Mr. Abracadabra

When I think about the consequences of

My actions...
        My ignorance...
                My lust...

That transpired all those years ago, I ache.
I ache for the beautiful and innocent little girl
Who was conceived, because she longed for
Something that she deserved but could not obtain.

If only I could begin again,
I would choose a man—a *real man...a husbandman*
To share this life—and not a *boy*friend.

I would choose someone who could
Transcend above oppositions and walk right
Into his demanded level of responsibility.

I would choose someone
Who had stored integrity and maturity
That cannot be shaken or compromised.

I would choose someone
Who doesn't create and hide behind
A mass of sorry-ass excuses
As to why...

NOT ANOTHER TEAR: MOVING FROM PAIN TO PURPOSE

His *daughter*
      His *blood*
           His *firstborn*
Is still—after all these years—left
Without a father.

How dare you desert your daughter?
You STUPID and SELFISH JERK!
You have no idea of the magnitude of
Hurt you've left behind.

Although you've written her off,
She still exists! And through my love
And God's love, she will come to realize
That she has more love than her little
Heart can hold.

And she will thrive and know that she is
Complete—beautifully designed—and is
Void of any inadequacies due to your absence.
For it is you who is incomplete and inadequate,
Void...of the true essence of manhood.

It Happened in the Bathroom

At work, clicking away at the keyboard,
I find grace and gratitude in the fact that
I have a job, income, a genuine likeness for
my co-workers, and the opportunity to support
our clientele.

However, I feel a steady rising swelling up
inside of me. It makes me think of April Showers
and Springtime.

With the kind of agony *(that usually only comes
with sorrow)* I suddenly feel a deep pain...as if
I've lost someone special.

I discreetly hurry off to the Lady's Room and
lock myself into one of the stalls.
Just as the door closes, water springs up and
out of me—forcing me to drop to my knees.
In this moment, it is crystal clear to me
that my soul is indeed, in mourning.

Suddenly, I fully understand the words of
one of the most beautiful and incomparable
poets to ever grace this planet, Dr. Maya Angelou,
who wrote: *"There is no greater agony than
bearing an untold story inside you."*

Weeping for my dreams deferred—for my
untold stories—I find myself agonizing
over all of my dreams that were eaten away

by fear, and those that died in *compromises,*
a serious lack of know-how, protests, and delays.

Following those tears, more spring up and out
of me—for all the other dreams that lay dormant
inside—eagerly waiting to be birthed.

My April Showers are swift and powerful,
albeit, brief. I pat my face and blow my nose,
as I slowly rise back onto my feet.

There, I remind myself that in April, it does
indeed rain, and the rain—accompany by
the nourishment of the sun—springs forth
beautiful flowers in due season.

It's a subtle reminder that my dreams still
have chances to bloom. They too—like my
tears—will one day spring up and out of me.

These dreams will not die in winter, nor in
compromises, protests, or further delays…
or by any other means.

#ItHappenedInTheBathroom
#MyDreamsSpringsForth
#NourishYourDreams

I Stayed Far Too Long

I stayed far too long in a career I had long outgrown,
far too long failing to plant the seeds I should have sown,
far too long in relationships that had lost their zest and
purpose, far too long in transit long after I should have taken
the off-ramp.

I stayed far too long developing action plans for a brighter
future only to never truly take action, far too long in the ugly
and repetitive cycle of indecision, far too long in a place that
no longer could contain my vision.

I stayed far too long living out my fear rather than my faith,
far too long chasing dollars instead of destiny, far too long
making dumb choices while denying the quiet still voice of
reason and raw gut instincts that live within to guide me.

I stayed far too long in silence—afraid of knowing and hearing the power and impact of my own voice.
Far too long *wishing* I had made a different choice.

I stayed far too long because convenience was the buy-in
rather than my own convictions. And convenience was not
merely convenient for convenience's sake.

I stayed far too long in convenience because it was familiar
and safe, albeit mundane and wrought with resentment,
detours, and unnecessary delays.

I stayed far too long because the *idea* of letting go *really* is the
hardest thing. For the *perception* of the outcome is often far

greater than the reality. Because the idea of letting go of something current to embrace something new and often unknown…can be *downright* frightening.

I stayed far too long, taking the risk of never having greater just so I could feel safe and secure in ignorant bliss—failing to fully evaluate and calculate the true risks.

I stayed far too long because in doing so, I wouldn't have to give up anything *now* to make room for something *later*—not realizing that my "later" would be greater than my "*right now.*"

Slowly hemorrhaging, my future was being aborted because I resorted to living life on *park*—somewhere between Complacency Boulevard and Fear Avenue.
If only I knew.

I stayed far too long, and now I must clear the path to my "later" by letting go of the "*right now.*" Although it's scary to start a new life chapter, *I must do this* because destiny is what I'm after!

Although it isn't convenient to do a complete overhaul of my life, I can't be bound to *this* moment in life. Therefore, I'm embracing the unknown *and* my convictions.

For the known no longer serves me. This level of misery is something I can no longer afford to bargain with. I must be wise but *swift* because time is of the essence.

I've learned my lessons…and before I run out of it…I want to know what it's like to live the life that God predestined me with.

I stayed far too long being *stiff*—stuck, stagnated, and deprived—living just to *survive* when purpose demands that I *thrive*!

I stayed far too long in mediocrity,
Far too long allowing bullies to get the best of me,
Far too long in resentment and un-forgiveness,
Far too long in mourning and depression,
Far too long failing to learn life's lessons,
Far too long in the trappings of victimization,
Far too long complaining about my situation,
Far too long living in my pain,
Far too long in poverty and shame,

Far too long dismissing my Creator—the one who holds my promise, my purpose, *my right now, and my later*!

Far too long treating myself unlovingly,
Far too long putting others before me,
Far too long retracing my steps repeatedly—only to trip over those mistakes again and again—*failing*, while watching others win!

I stayed far too long...but I'm *done* with being stuck!
And I don't believe in luck!

Destiny driven—is now how I'm living—so passivity move over! *You're over!*

I am taking back the driver's seat...
for my future...awaits!

It Isn't About Me

This isn't about me.
It's all about my seed and how
She longed to break free
From her wounds, her hurts...
And sometimes...even from me.

You see, her heart bled
Because she yearned for an
Unfulfilled need, a need that
Kept her in bondage instead of
Freed.

How did this happen?
I can only reminisce.
But if I'm not completely honest,
I'd be remiss.

In the words I've spoken out in anger
Left a token of ever-present danger.

In the beatings I gave
To try and make her behave,
In the unsung anger and my fiery rage...
They all became uncaged...and there
In silence she sat center stage.

In the many times he wasn't there...
Your father...who never cared.
For fifteen years not one thing he did

To show you that he loved you, kid.
I know it hurts to the core of your soul…
Unspoken words that are yet to be told.

I just want you be strong…and to do your
Best. Don't start out like me and turn your
Life into a complete mess.

I guess…all of those things I said and did
Were some bizarre way of trying to save
You, kid.

Oftentimes you felt like a bullet train
Derailing off the tracks, so I engaged in
By-any-means-necessary tactics to try to
Bring you back.

For I saw where you were going—you
Only saw where you were at.

NOT ANOTHER TEAR: MOVING FROM PAIN TO PURPOSE

Because She Yearned

Their mama left without hesitation,
Hurried out the door in fact
To embrace her *desire* for freedom—
Clothes *already* packed.
She left *everything* behind,
Including those whom she bore—
To live as a new-generation kind of whore.

She doesn't just sell her body for money—
She also sells her soul, honey!
Drugging and drinking,
Clubbing and winking,
Stealing and dealing.

Over there on Broad Street, the dope
Dealers make a killing off her every day.
Death is instilled within her eyes
As her insides slowly decay...

Due to the needles she injects and the
Damaging effects of the white powder that
Viciously erodes her ravaged temple...

Dealing with crying babies was much
More dignified and simple.

Cops around here know her very well
As many times as she's been to jail.
Prostituting by night—showing off her

Ninety-eight-pound physique—
What's left of what *used* to be
One hundred and fifty-three.

High as a kite with both feet unsteadily
Mounted on the ground—forcing herself
To forget about the little children left
Motherless on the other side of town.

Although in bondage to her own demise,
This *twisted* sense of freedom feels right in
Her eyes.

They tell me she was running from something
In her past...but doesn't she know, *you can't*
Outrun your own looking-glass?

And what about those babies, left

Hungry,
Scared,
And
Alone?

Who's going to teach them how to deal with
Skeletons of their own?

Who's going to rock them and put them to sleep?
Who's going to comfort them when their little eyes
Weep?

Who's going to be Mother?

NOT ANOTHER TEAR: MOVING FROM PAIN TO PURPOSE

Who's going to be Friend?
Who's going to pick up the pieces and fix what's
Just been broken?

Who's going to love them and wipe the abandonment
Stains from their now-scarred hearts and brains?
Will it be you?

Ashamed

Unexpected blessing
From day one, you kept me guessing
Didn't realize it then because
I was only seventeen
With no education—years of struggling
And knew *little* patience.

Barely standing against the wind,
I knew nothing back then!
Baby, I won't try and pretend
That life was *fine.*

Many nights I cried a mother's cry,
For I had no teacher—feared for you
And I—wondered, *"How will I reach her?"*

No mother or father to ask about the
Experience of parenting—
Everything was just a guessing game.
I was ashamed…

That I knew nothing back then.

Unnecessary Struggle

She wakes up some mornings wondering…
How will I make it through the day?
Single mother on her own trying to make
A better way.

Looking from place to place,
With no help in sight.
Daddy walked out—leaving
Mother and babies to fight,
Daddy—that isn't right!

A mother is left wondering which direction to turn
After birthing your baby girl and your newborn son
Just to see your back as you cowardly turn and run.

Devastation in their minds because you've left
Them all behind, with:

Daycare, hospital bills, and everything in between.
They cry out for some relief, but there's none to be
Seen.

…And you call *yourself* a man?

Good Morning, God

How dare I inhale your oxygen?
How dare I dwell upon your earth?
How dare I drink from your *endless* well
Without ever acknowledging your worth?

How could I be so selfish?
How could I be so unkind?
How could I fail to recognize you,
For this life you gave of mine?

Long have I ignored you,
Like some stranger in distant sight—
Only to recognize you when I am
Experiencing plight.

Please accept my apology.
Please don't refuse this request,
For I now know that without you
My life *cannot* be blessed!

So now to you, I say I'm sorry.
To you, I say hello.
To you, I say thank you
Wherever I go.

To you, God, I say...*GOOD MORNING.*

Never, Never, Never

It's important to own your story,
Including your own mistakes—
And how they may have deeply affected
Others along the way.

Do not minimize the damage
Or try to explain your past away, simply
To make excuses.

You lose respect this way
And a real opportunity to grow,
And since the absence of growth is
Death...*well*, you get my point.

Apologize. Ask for forgiveness, and
Forgive yourself.

Take real ownership, and work hard to
Make amends, but after awhile,
You must assess the miles and the hard work
You've put in to make right, your wrong.

But,

Never, never, never
Permit others to hold you hostage to the past.
Your story is still being written,
So it's the present that needs you now.
Therefore, live in the vast space of *this* moment

More wisely, intentionally, lovingly, and
Unapologetically, while making progressive steps
To be better than you were on yesterday.

Never, never, never
Deny yourself the freedom and the right
To grow past your pain, past your sorrow, past your
Regrets, or past the mistakes you've made.

Never, never, never
Give in to the impulse to collapse your chin
Into your chest with cast-down eyes—
Fixated on the ground—beset with shame.

Come…into *this* moment, learn, grow, love, forgive,
And live!

This Thing We Call Love

Plastic

You tried to play with my emotions.

Pulled strings that I didn't even know I had—
Twisted my heart and left it broken—
Took my good loving and used it for bad.

Treated me as if I was some cheaply made factory toy—
Designed exclusively for your amusement—
Which explains why you came off like a GI Joke—

When I came out of my slumber... and woke...up
To your lies...and the stench of your burn...

...I should've known your love was plastic.

I Am Home

I am not the Freeway
You merge onto whenever
You want to go on a quick drive
—Only to get off at the next exit.

I am the driveway you enter
When you know that you are home,
After a long hard day at work.
I am both ends of your spectrum—
Including the middle.

I am the period at the end of your
Sentences—without question.

I am the lyrics in your song.
I am Proverbs 31.
And I am Ruth!

I am not the woman name Jezebel.
I am Deborah; I am truth.

I am the water you bathe in
To soak your cares away;

I am the ocean you swim in
And the Spring you drink from.

So, don't come to me whispering
Sweet nothings in my ear—only
When you're thirsty.

I am your life-line—your life-time.
I am, "Let me take you home to
Meet mama."

I am wedding bells in September—
Your other half.

I am kisses at noon and at breakfast time.
I am dances under the moon; I am sunshine.

I am homemade buttermilk biscuits and gravy.
I am, "Let's make love at sunrise."

I am Filet Mignon, broccoli, and perfectly
Seasoned mash potatoes—at the candle-lit
Dinner table.

My love is *solid, good...and, stable.*
It fills you up—and with it—you shall
Never...grow hungry.

For, I...am home.

Gone are the days of the Young Girl with Blues

You thought I was still that young
Girl with blues—gullible and bruised
—The one you could use…

The one who wore her heart on her
Sleeve—desperate for love and ready
To cleave—onto anyone resembling
The embodiment of true love…
Even when it was clearly, counterfeit.

I must admit, 'you tried it,' but you
Need to quit—because I will *burn* you
Like gasoline and matches…

And will discard the remnants of
Your ashes in the belly of the driest
And darkest Well…and forget you
Ever existed.

For, gone are the days of the
Young girl with blues—that you
Could use—only to leave shattered,
In the aftermath.

Boys Who Chase the Wind

Boys, disguised as men…who chase after
The elusive wind—because
They think the grass is greener
On the other side of that which
Blows—ends up getting
Swept up, by hurricanes.

Poison

I grew immune to your
Sensual touches, come-hither
Gazes, and tantalizing wet
Kisses—that were packaged ever-so
Beautifully—wrapped in shiny gifts,
False praises, and in the insincere
Words, "I love you."

All disguised as remedies—
When in reality—you were
Nothing but poison.

Trapped in Between Loving and Longing

Trapped in between
Loving and longing—
You came along and kissed
Me in places that had long been
Deaden.

My heart had become a forgotten
Buried treasure—buried under
The fallout from false promises of
Exclusivity, and adorning love that
Would last forever.

But your love was clever.

You touched me in places
I never knew existed.
You showed me love and
Gave me hope—had me
Believing in my own ambitions
...And in us.

With great patience and
Well-crafted precision, you tore down
My walls and inhibitions.

I thought to myself:
"Finally, I am receiving real love this time.
I am worthy of real love this time."

You were my 'next time.'
You were my 'this time'—
My 'lifetime'—only to become
My 'last time'…

Because, just as suddenly as you
Appeared—you vanished without
Explanation—and now I sit here,
Triggered.

I love you but I hate you.
I hate you for waking up that part
Of me only to kill it again.

Do you know what it is like to
Come alive—to be awakened, and to
Love again—after your heart has
Been broken…one too many times…
Only to die again?

Why wasn't I…enough?

I gave you my trust…
And you broke me with it.

I'm Sorry

When love betrays you for
The last time like the many
"Last times" before, it becomes
An overwhelmingly heart-wrenching
Task to endure.

And to strip down—to bear the
Burden of looking at yourself
In the mirror—to say to the
Woman who's staring back at you, in tears:

"I'm sorry for the mass pain I've
Caused by being a fool...again.

For getting *sucked in* again,
For *loving* again,
For *trusting* again,
For *longing*...again,
For being a *touched*
Woman...again—*broken again*—
By the one whom I let
Touch you, again..."

It is devastating.

When Love is Plagiarized

This love thing doesn't have to hurt
And true love never does.

If only I can somehow escape from this
Fleeting counterfeit version that always
Comes—dressed up in camouflage…

It chases me down when I'm least
Expecting—when I'm standing still
With my heart concealed—carefully
Tucked away because it has already
Been broken.

I resist, repeatedly—not wanting to
Feel the pitter patter in my heart,
Or the dancing butterflies in the pit
Of my stomach—that's often followed by the
Crashing sounds and thunderous pounds
Of my fragmented heart being shattered,
Again…and the crushing of my butterflies' wings
That causes them to lose their dance
And I, my hope after the counterfeit loses its disguise.

…When true love, has been plagiarized.

When Nightmares Become Real

He touched my lips with his fingertips
And told me to hush, as he pressed
His freeing hand against the curve of
My hips. *I blushed.*

And there in silence, with my heart
Racing at paces of unbelievable speed—
Anxiously waiting to be freed—
He gently kissed me about my neck.
And in that instance, I felt regret.

Then suddenly, I burst into flames,
And woke up screaming his name—
And devastated—only to later learn that
My heart would get burned, and be
Terrorized...

Because true love, had once again, been
Plagiarized.

This Thing We Call Love

Love is not...
Jealousy,
Envy, or
Strife.

Love doesn't leave you wounded
And scarred for life!

Love *builds up*!
It doesn't tear down a life.

Love is not a fist beating upon your frame.
Love is not the calling of cruel and nasty names.
Love...caresses and protects you from harm.

With *love,*
Baby, you don't need *any* protective armor on
That shields you from the bruising that he often
Leaves behind.

Love brings joy and a peace of mind.

Love!

Love is not sadness or a destructive, raving madness.
Love is a medicine that fills a soul with *gladness*!
This thing you're calling love...

IT'S OUT OF CONTROL.

Love!

Baby, love can't be this cold.

Although you've sat in silence and in tumultuous fear,
You must gather the nerve to reclaim your power
And escape from out of there because...

Love!

Love is not beating, cheating, or misleading.
Love doesn't make you feel like a trapped dog
Wounded and bleeding!

Love doesn't leave you breathless due to a strong
Hand squeezing your neck.

Love is not controlling nor fills a heart with regret.

Love!

Beloved...are you *sure* this is *love*?
Somebody ought to check this.

Because this thing you're calling love...*baby,*
It ain't love...it's *raving* MADNESS!!!!!!!

Alone

Being alone can hurt so bad.
Feeling that it is you against the world
No one to stand by your side
Through the tumultuous lows
Or the mountain highs.

Want to run and tell someone
How was your day,
But there's nobody there to listen.
This is no way to exist...

Because everybody
Needs somebody
To love, to talk to, and...to kiss.
And, baby, that's why I long for you
At the setting of the sun
And at the rising of a new one.

And when I go home,
The shadows of your footprints roam.
They *still* haunt me.
I fought to win at love
But instead, I ended up *losing*.

Baby, baby, oh, baby!
But I can't waste my time
With a man with an unmade-up mind.
One day you want me, and the next day you don't.
So, I had to give you your walking papers

Even though it hurts me so!

Now, every night being alone
Is not a lonely plight,
'Cause sometimes I like being by my damn self,
But there are many nights I need to be held.

And baby, that's why I long for you
At the setting of the sun
And at the rising of a new one.

I Want a Man!

I...want a man!
But not the kind who grins and lies
While hiding behind a deceitful disguise,
But one who's self-confident and has
Integrity—one who, when he speaks,
I'm inclined to believe.

I...want a man!
But not the kind who rants and raves
And turns my blue skies into grays,
But one who has encountered peace
And the joy it brings...one who,
When he enters the room,
Makes my spirit sing.

I...want a man!
One whom I don't have to share
With all of you *other* sisters
Or...*brothers* out there,
But one who I can call my own
And not one who's been put on *loan*.

I...want a man!
Who doesn't play *childish* games.
Unless I'm mistaken, I've only
Birthed *one* child from this body
Through intense labor and pain.

NOT ANOTHER TEAR: MOVING FROM PAIN TO PURPOSE

No!
I...want a man!
Who's mature in all of his ways,
Not one who I have to make
And mold like back in the
Playground days.

I...want a man!
But not the kind who sees me
Just as his woman or wife.
The *world* and even the church nowadays
Are filled with too many of both types
Who tend to come and go.

So...I want a man
Who knows he's king in my life
And in his knowing—knows I am
Queen and *wife*!

I...want a man!
But not the kind who sits high
And looks low—*I already have that
Man, and his name, is God.*

No! I want a man who sits low and
Looks high.

I...want a man!
But *not*...right at this time.
Just putting in an *early* request
Because he won't be easy to find.
There are so many particulars...

Those characteristics and features that
My soul yearns to have in this
Extraordinary masculine creature.

So, I'll be patient and continue
To work hard on me because what I desire
In that man—*that* must I also be.
But in the meantime…, *who am
I kidding?*

I…want a man!

...And More of This Thing We Call Love

Uncontrollable

It drives me crazy when you think you know what's
Best for me and try to control my choices.

I am uncontrollable!

Regardless of how long it's been since you came
Along or how well you think you know me,
Remember, I've known me a heck of a lot longer
Than, you've known me.

I live, eat, breathe, think, dream, sing, have birthed a
Child—hell, I've even ran a mile or two—have
Failed and succeeded, loved and hated, prayed and
Fasted, forgiven and sinned, laughed, cried, and been
Elated in *this* skin!

Made love on the countertop and slow danced to
Prince's "Purple Rain" and dropped it like it was hot to
LL's hip-hop!

Laughed and cried, flourished with pride, drank
Wine and exotic teas, permed, blow-dried, went all-
Natural, and even sported a weave.

Feared for my own destiny but found the courage to
Believe. Eat Chilean Seabass and Macaroni and Cheese.
Have fought off attackers—destiny's would-be hijackers.
And write, form, and transform basic words into powerful
Poems.

I am uncontrollable!

You've tried rather daringly—and need I say—
Quite ignorantly, to convince yourself as well
As me, that you know me better than I know myself!
This is absurd.

For I *live* in this skin!

You'll find yourself highly disappointed trying to
'Box' me in.

I was living and thriving before
You *ever* came on the scene, so please, love me for me,
Or leave.

Before you even attempt to call me your woman,
Please know that I am my own woman first.

I have no need to be rebirthed—and I know my worth:
Molded out of destiny's hands—given life, uniqueness,
And purpose at God's command. I was complete and
Validated *then*.

So if you chose to stay, please don't do so with the
Intent of trying to change, or control me.

I am uncontrollable!

Now, having said that, I am not some inflexible object
Of your affection and desire, because I don't mind
Bending, baby: I said *bending*.

I don't mind compromising or meeting you halfway,
And I don't even mind making sacrifices…for anyone
Worth loving, is clearly worth giving up a *little*
Something for: I said a *little* something.

You see, although I am willing to make *some*
Sacrifices, don't ever expect me to *become* the sacrifice.

And…and I don't need you to be my daddy.
I just want you to be *my* man.

Now baby, if you can understand, and roll with
That…then let's slow things down and *re…begin*.

Tsunami Love

My heart is so heavy,
I feel it bursting at the seams.
A tsunami river of love flowing...
It far exceeds a mere stream.

Loving hard with no regard,
This thing I feel is unstoppable.
No levees to hold it down—
Controlling it is improbable.

Got me drowning,
Sinking hard like a stone—
Next breath unattainable—
Forced in a danger zone.

One of the Greatest Rhythms God Has Ever Made

I lay upon his chest to rest,
And to be caressed, and I know
In this moment—I am
Incredibly blessed to hear—
Life beating so powerfully
Inside of him.

His heartbeat is one of the
Greatest rhythms God has
Ever made.

It plays…like the rhythmic
Sound of drum-beats in Autumn,
And dazzles like Angelou's Poetry,
Savion's Tap, and Gillespie's Jazz.

Chills my bones like
Wintertime and snowflakes—
And like Prince on the
Electric guitar.

It revives me like Springtime,
Flowers, and rain.

His heartbeat plays so
Beautifully, and is breathtaking.

Like Summertime—and Hot
Chocolate coated with Marsh
Mellows—it warms every
Fiber of my existence, from
The inside, out.

Like the flowing river—and like
The coolest breeze cascading across
My skin—it calms me.

His heartbeat is one of the
Greatest rhythms God has ever
Made, and I wish for it…to *never*
Stop beating.

Children Are People, Too

Children are people, too.
If you want to *break* a child's spirit,
Curse him out and belittle him.
Slap him in the face...punch him.
Give him cause to feel worthless and unloved.

If you want to *shatter* a child's self-esteem
And dim the light in her eyes—tell her that
She is stupid, ugly, or dumb. Bully her, essentially.
But...if you want to *raise* a child, as well as
His or her spirit and self-confidence,
Then tell your children what a *loving* parent does...

Tell him...tell her...the absolute truth—that they
Are the product of divine greatness—and are
Intelligent, beautiful, important, special...loved!
And when you get through telling them—show them.

For you are *your* children's foundation and *first*
Light, but if the *foundation* by which they stand
Upon is compromised, and if their *first light* fails to
Shine ever so brightly upon them *(because the light*
Itself is flickering and is succumbing to the darkness
Of its own frustration and rage),

Then what becomes of the hopes, the dreams, the
Confidence, the sense of self-worth, the security, the
Ideas, the spirit, and the possibilities of *that* child?
Embedded in the minds of our children should not

Be the handed-down ashes of regretful and misguided
Parenting but rather the blessing of knowing that
They are greatly loved, honored, and respected by
Those who gave them life.

I Never Thought

You were so young and vibrant and
Had the world at your feet.
You had the sweetest spirit
Beyond belief.

Life changing seeds you sowed
In many lives, even those you didn't know.
Why did you have to go?

So full of light—shining bright in dark places—
You turned many frowns into smiling faces.
The magic of you was impossible for imitations.
A beautiful and authentic original, you were.

Never thought that you'd leave me here;
I thought I'd be the first to go.

Ashes to Ashes...dust to dust—
Unbelievable sadness you left in all of us—
When you left us *suddenly*.
How can this be?

The essence of you were perhaps far too grand
To stay here any longer.
Your presence made us stronger.
You were too kind.
You're flying now.

For a while, we had an angel too, and that angel
Was you.

Rebirth

When we're together, it's like a rebirthing
Because all things become new...again,
When I'm with him.

It's refreshing to see his smile and to feel
His essence, and to know his embrace.
He doesn't think so highly of himself and
He doesn't take himself too seriously.

He thinks I'm delirious because I express
How captivating and stimulating he
Has made my mind.

He can't comprehend the why.

His humility is one of the reasons why
I love him like I do.

So humble and kind...
And when I'm not with him, constant
Imagery of his tender kisses lingers in my mind.
My heart is filled, and is connected with his—
They're intertwined.

Often told that our lovemaking drains him
Because I work marathons...so when I'm gone it will
Sustain him—giving him substance—all that his body
Yearns for and needs.

Together, our bodies are freed...to meet the
Highest of pleasure.

No inhibitions or insecurities to hold captive
Our unexploited treasures...

...But it's not all about sex...*really*.

Confessions

It's been a long time for us—a lifetime actually—since our eyes last met and we hugged each other goodbye that evening in front of the Greyhound Bus Station.

You had me at our first hello…all those years ago, but you *never* knew it. Those midnight conversations and holding hands till dawn underneath stretches of stars and moonlight—that danced into the beat of morning—I can never forget.

Oh, how we laughed, kissed, hugged, and talked—and then talked some more—baby, it didn't matter to you that you didn't score.

Like a combination lock, we *just* clicked—vibed together like a candle on a candlestick. And the country-boy charm that you tastefully adorned still *turns* me on.

Now the Jackson Five's "Good Times" is my *favorite* song.

Damn…I want you! *Confessions*:

And since I am confessing, here is one more confession— I hope you don't mind: When I talked to you the other day, those feelings of the past were past no more. They hit me hard like a tsunami unearthed from the ocean's floor.

Immersed under, I could barely catch my breath when I saw your face and then heard your voice. Suddenly thrust back in time, when time stood still, and, like Baby Face, boy, you've got that *whip appeal*!

It was you who woke up the flaming desire in me.
It was something about the way you inspired me.
Baby, you *grooved* me. And without ever touching me, you *touched* me all over!

Damn, I want you! *Confessions*:

In silence I've loved you for such a long time—a lifetime, actually. It is you who ignited all that I'm feeling—the flutters, flickers, and the flames...got me wanting to carry a child for you boy, and share your last name.

All those years ago, like a whisper, the flame has been flickering in the distance. Seeing your face and hearing your voice was overwhelming the other day.

It provoked dreams, schemes, and all sorts of feelings and thoughts, and then, I dreamed of you:

In my subconscious, my heart pulsated nervously with every delicate stroke of your fingertips—that you
cascaded with great precision, up and down my spine.

For my body knew not this language—it left me tongue-tied. This unspoken tongue—so foreign, I lay at your mercy... *breathless*.

Tenderness was your kiss at the arch of my back. Ascended, strong and powerful were your hands that clutched the curve of my thighs.

I was a kept prisoner of your love, but baby, with gladness I wanted to be your delicate songbird because I didn't want to be free. I didn't want to fly away.
I wanted to stay.

And…and if I was with you now, we'd make love till dawn with bodies in motion—channeling the waves of the sea and panting to the rhythm of sunrise!

And we'd lie content in the sensual pleasures of morning as husband and wife—with wetness between my thighs—as your mojo gets baptized in the waters of my womanhood.

Feels so…damn good!

And *somewhere* in between the oohs and the aahs—
we are reborn.

Damn, I want you! *Confessions*

What Defines a Man?

Some will argue and toil with the question,

What defines a man?

Is it the masculinity of his frame?
Or is it the echoes that resound in a woman's heart
At the mere mentioning of his name?

Is it the strength in his hands
That makes him the *epitome* of man?

What defines a man?

Is it his *smooth* talking and, like a summer's *breeze*,
Is it his *cool* walking?

Or is it the amount of digits that's inked across his
Paycheck, or is it the ability for him to stand *erect*?

What defines a man?

Although I'm a woman, here's my stand:

Thousands have strayed
After they have laid—leaving little children
Fatherless and afraid.

Angry little boys searching for the good in them
While wounded grown men are hurting over what

Could have been.

And the teenage girls are desperately seeking for love in
All the *wrong* places—trying hard to fill the void of their
Daddies' missing faces—by lying on their backs, hearts
Bleeding and cracked—utterly broken!

They're willing to sell out for *anybody's* love
And affection as a token.

But though these thousands of *"want to be men"*
Have strayed after they have laid…

Real men like some of you have stayed—
Perhaps not *unafraid* and without having your
Share of bad days—I know it's hard.

And that's why I extend my regards!
In *spite* of your plight, like warriors you fight *daily*
For your family, faith, and employment and for
Some respect, love, and simple enjoyment.

You real men don't make excuses or tell fairy tales.
You honor the lives you helped to conceive
By supplying *every* one of their needs:

Emotionally,
Spiritually,
Physically, *and*
Financially.

That's what makes you the epitome!
So to define a man as best as I can,

As a woman in this land,

Is to say,
He doesn't flee from his responsibilities—
He stands!

Distant Lover

One month
One week
One day
One hour
One moment
One second
One *breath*...

At a time, I stand and wait for you—counting down
The time when I can see you again.

With a heart so intertwined with yours, mine
Beats in alignment with your heart's rhythm—
In anticipation to capture yet another glimpse
Of your essence.

Truly I'm invested. And my mind...it's so entrenched
With constant thoughts and prayers of and for you.

My distant lover—

Long have I ceased fighting against these feelings because
Baby, I simply adore you.

And though I still don't quite understand the longevity or
The gravity, given our absence, I know there is no other
Place upon this earth I'd rather be—except gripped up in
The clutches of your arms or standing next to you as we
Travel along this path of exploration—

NOT ANOTHER TEAR: MOVING FROM PAIN TO PURPOSE

This ain't no damn act of desperation!

But I must admit, I hunger and thirst for liberation
'Cause, baby, I want to be free to love you the way a
Woman in love ought to—without these countless zip
Codes standing between us—got me feeling like I want
To combust because I miss you so much. And this thing
Between us goes *far* beyond lust.

I miss your gorgeous smile and the way you wrinkle up
Your forehead when you are engaged in thought.

I miss sitting on the couch, with my leg dangling over
Yours like a participle, while watching funny bloopers on
YouTube.

I miss you coming up behind me—wrapping your body
All around mine as I inhale the sexiness of your...aura.
And just like the poem, "Rhythm in My Skin," your kisses,
Whispers, and blows tingle my bones...causing my
Insides to begin harmonizing songs.

I miss lying down with you and having your head in my
Lap—as I gently caress your crown while you
Passionately rub your hands up and down my leg, while
We take turns falling asleep watching a movie on
Television.

I miss giving you a *hot* bubble bath underneath the dim
Lights of scented candles with the echoes of classic jazz
Playing in the background—washing your body from
Head to toe, as you get fresh with me.

I miss giving you a full-body massage afterward.
I have this thing about relaxing you, but honestly, baby,
It's all an excuse just to touch you because somehow
Touching you…relaxes me.

In those simple moments of pleasure, I am one with you.
But the truth is, I get scared sometimes, as I wonder if
Destiny will someday truly make you mine. They say love
Is blind and that the truest of love is hardest to find.
So even in the face of this mass distance and fear, I stand
Without reluctance to love you, because *I love you*!

And if I end up with shattered pieces of my heart falling
From my trembling hands, I won't ever regret loving you
Because with certainty, my distant lover, for a time you
Were *my* man!

I can *stand* knowing that I loved you with all of who
I am—withholding nothing!

And, oh, yeah, I love it when you call me early in the
Morning, noonday, at dinnertime, or even in the middle
Of the night, asking me silly questions like:
"Baby, are you asleep?"

You're such a damn night freak.

Distant lover!

Oh, how I long to love you again and again and again
In between, under and over, out of, and even on top of
The sheets!

Because I don't mind being your freak!
E*very* day of the week!

I stand here loving you across zip codes and state lines.
Risking it *all* because they say *long-distance lovers have
Rarely stood the test of time.*

And maybe that's true, but like Maze—Featuring Frankie
Beverly, my distant lover, "I Can't Get Over You."
I...I can't get over you.

Catching Eyes

Catching eyes,
So beautifully created with a touch of perfection—
Image like holiness in the midst of dawn
Underneath the glare of sunlight.

So...supple and hypnotic and unsurprisingly
Suggestive.

If my movement should gravitate to the right,
Catching eyes are magnetically transcending
Upon my frame.

If my movement gravitates to the left,
Those catching eyes gravitate the same.

Why do you stare at me, I wonder?
Is it my heavenly beauty that entices you—
That causes your wanting eyes to sparkle
Like heaven's moon?

Or is it my tune?

Do my thighs sing to you like Marvin Gay?
"Let's get it on."

When my hips glide from side to side,
Do you hear that old eighties tune?
"I wanna ride."

Or perhaps it is the shape of my designer
Legs that provokes those catching eyes to
Stare and beg.

Or maybe it's my...hmmm?
Rarely do I see catching eyes catching me!
I possess more than what your beautifully
Human-shaped eyes can see.

Catching eyes,
Longing to break the veil of my temple...
So caught in what may be obtained
From my heavenly designed frame.

Do I *dress* to entice you?
Do I *strut* to allure you?
Do I *glide* with intent to one day climb upon
Your throne, allowing you entrance into my
Holy veil? No!

I *dress*. I *strut*. And I *glide*
With class as I walk down the street
With *no* intentions to throw away my virginity.

You see, I learned the hard way
Never to *cast* my pearls before swine.
For what God has given me is precious
And divine.

So with my chin lifted toward the heavens,
I smile with songs of freedom echoing in
My heart because I *finally* realized my value...

Wish I had from the start.
So if you see me again walking confidently
Down the street, know that it's not you who
I seek. But...

Don't be afraid to smile and speak.
Just be sure that your *catching eyes*
Catch mine, and not the thing that I
Set on that lingers...*behind.*

Rhythm of My Pace

Slow and steady, baby,
Is the rhythm of my pace.
I'm sipping on your love, slowly.
Yeah, like a fine, supple wine, I drink.

You command my full attention.
Oh, did I forget to mention…
That you're complex and alluring?

You've got me adoring every facet of you,
As I gladly take my time to study your intentions—
As well as your body and your mind, and, dare I say,
Even your *swagger*, hard.

But, *slow*…and steady, baby,
Is the rhythm of my pace.
Sipping on your love *slowly*,
Like a fine, supple wine, oh, yeah…I drink.

He Was Born Into This Rhythm

La bella (Spanish)
That brotha was bad.
That brotha was bad.
That brotha was bad.
That brotha was bad.
He was *born* into this rhythm

Utshkuski 1 (Japanese)
That brotha was bad.
That brotha was bad.
That brotha was bad.
That brotha was bad.
He was *born* into this rhythm

La belle (French)
That brotha was bad.
That brotha was bad.
That brotha was bad.
That brotha was bad.
He was *born* into this rhythm

Il bello (Italian)
That brotha was bad.
That brotha was bad.
That brotha was bad.
That brotha was bad.
He was *born* into this rhythm

Sundar ek (Hindi)

That brotha was bad.
That brotha was bad.
That brotha was bad.
That brotha was bad.
He was *born* into this rhythm

The Beautiful One (English)
That brotha was bad.
That brotha was bad.
That brotha was bad.
That brotha was bad.

Like a fine wine
He got even better with time—
So mellow—he captivated the mind.
He was *born* into this rhythm.

He was *born* into this rhythm—
He decimated the masses.
Those that came before and after him
He smashed them—just ask them.

He was the epitome of *'Purple Badness!'*
4/21/16 created world sadness!

He played twenty-seven instruments—
A bona fide genius and a personification
Of brilliance and resilience—and let's
Not talk about his sex appeal that
Thrilled…us across *every* color dimension.

When he entered a room

He commanded undivided attention.
He was the world's iconic treasure—
An indisputable legend, but *authenticated!*
A *real* beast on stage and he never wavered!
And though some tried, they couldn't
Duplicate him.

He was like a chameleon in the way he
Shared his brilliance—that's why we celebrate him!
He stroked instruments to perfection—
Like a well-versed lover, he wrecked them
Only to resurrect them.

He created melodies—potent like 'gasms'
That evoked spasms that left us
Damn near lifeless—*yet* craving for more,
We *had* to have him.
He's *still adored.*

Even though he's now lifeless—
His presence still lives on.
Undeniably...unrepeatable—
Gone but not forgotten—
Undeletable!

His essence is like poetry—
Artistic and well-versed—unrehearsed.
He can *never truly be gone.*

Created by the Creator—
A divine melody—
Who played his position well.

And if his genius was a crime
He'd be music's Capon but *never* captured!

He was *born* into this rhythm
He...he was *born* into this rhythm
He...he was born into this rhythm
That's why we still...dance to his rhythm
Dance...dance to his rhythm
That's why we still...dance to his rhythm

That brotha was bad.
That brotha was bad.
That brotha was bad.
That brotha was bad.

That brotha was bad.
That brotha was bad.
That brotha was bad.
That brotha was baddddd.

(In memoriam of Prince Rogers Nelson, RIP.
Forever your fan...and adorer too. ~ Hollingsworth)

#HeWasBornIntoThisRhythm

Baddddd

Last night, I saw him dancing in my dreams.
His feet moved as fast as lightning,
lightning
lightning
lightning

Hot like fire,
fire
fire
fire

as he moved to the rhythm,
to the rhythm
to the rhythm
to the rhythm of...

ancient old melodies
combined with today's
contemporary hip-hop philosophies.

That brotha was bad.
That brotha was bad.
That brotha was bad.
That brotha was bad.

I saw him dancing in my dreams
strong, tall, masculine, and
yet sensual to the touch,
caused my skin to melt like butter,

like butter
like butter
like butter
like butter

Too hot to handle,
he, a roaring flame—I a meager candle.
His moves burned through my flesh,

Smoking hot!
setting my bones ablaze,
ablaze
ablaze
ablaze

So deep did it penetrate…
even causing our ancestors to
stand up and give him praise,
praise
praise
praise

That brotha was bad.
That brotha was bad.
That brotha was bad.
That brotha was bad.

I saw him dancing in my dreams.
Powerfully and eloquently he did flow—
exuding rhythms as music gushed from his skin—
I nearly drown a thousand times trying to swim
in my failed attempt to flow with him,

flow with him
flow with him
flow with him

That brotha was bad.
That brotha was bad.
That brotha was bad.
That brotha was bad.

That brotha was bad.
That brotha was bad.
That brotha was bad.
That brotha was *baddddd*!

The Allures of Darkness

Standing at the Edge of Midnight

It's dark…and like a black heap,
I am standing on the edge of night,
Scattered.

Psychologically and
Emotionally battered,
Physically weakened…
Spiritually shattered.

I hate myself…
And the life I've endured
Sickened with grief, but
I find no cure.

What is it that make
Me want to flee:
From my past
From my history
From me?

The Allures of Darkness

Passivity is not the nature of alluring darkness,
Though it sets in silence deceitfully still and
Cunningly quiet, at the core of its hollowed roots—
Lurking in obscurity *and* insecurity is an utter
Coldness that deviously waits to suffocate
Even the smallest glimmer of light.

Frustrated in its own darkness,
Satisfied in its own discord, *yet* content with nothing—
Except to eliminate the glorious light that seeks to
Shine ever so brightly.

For it holds no dreams, possesses no cares,
And expresses no sorrows.
It possesses a madness of multiple dimensions.
The sane will never grasp its incomprehensible,
Vain intentions.

But with all of its trickery, allures, and woes
Light persists—boldly and glaringly shining in all
Of its brilliance and splendor—cutting deeply through
The seemingly inescapable darkness.

Utter darkness will never *take over*,
Suffocate, eradicate, or hold hostage the
Relentless, tenacious, and the divinely powerful spirit
That embodies the very essence of light.

For just as in the night sky, regardless of

NOT ANOTHER TEAR: MOVING FROM PAIN TO PURPOSE

The intensity of the darkness,
The moon and millions of stars never
Cease to shine—never giving in to the
Alluring darkness—always standing,
Though a few stars may fall; so it is with us.

We are the light, and together we *all* shine.
And if by chance your light becomes dim
And you find yourself slowly succumbing to the
Allures of darkness, strike a match—light a candle,
And quickly find your way back to your rightful place
Among the beautiful light that you are.

They Call...But I Don't Answer

They call me
Ugly,
But I call me
Beautiful!

They call me
Cursed
Because I am dark,
But I call me
Blessed!

For I bear the mark—
Kissed and *caressed*
By God's own sun.

They call me
Nigger,
But I call me
Queen!

They call me
Easy,
But I call me
Worth the wait!

They call me
Defeated,
But I call me
Winner!

NOT ANOTHER TEAR: MOVING FROM PAIN TO PURPOSE

They call me
Inferior,
But I call me
Fierce!

They call me
Worthless,
But I call me
Treasure!

They call me
Wounded,
But I call me
Healed!

They call me
Poor,
But I call me
Rich!

They call me
Victim,
But I call me
Victorious!

They call me
Weak,
But I call me
Warrior!

They call me
The infamous "B" word,

But I call me
Woman!

They call me a
Mistake...
But God calls me
Purpose!

What! Are they calling you?
And do you *dare*...answer?

They Call...But He Doesn't Answer, Either

They call him
Inferior,
But he calls himself
Equal!

They call him
Incompetent,
But he calls himself
Clever!

They call him
Boy,
But he calls himself
Man!

They call him
Cunning,
But he calls himself
Credible!

They call him
Defeated,
But he calls himself
Conqueror!

They call him
Complacent,

But he calls himself
Accomplished!

They call him
A thug,
But he calls himself
A law-abiding citizen!

They call him
A Player,
But he calls himself
A man of honor!

They call him a
"Baby's daddy,"
But he calls himself
A husband and a
Father to his children!

They call him
A minority,
But he calls himself
The majority!

They call him
Hateful,
But he calls himself
Loving!

They call him
Damned,
But he calls himself
Destined!

They call him
Many *derogatory* names
To try to define his worth,
Yet he does not answer
Because he knows the
Purpose of his birth.

Destined by design—only God can define
His name...***do you know your name?***

On the Verge!

I'm on the verge
Of a *melt*down,
So don't bring me bad news.
I'm on the verge of a meltdown.
Bring me some *good* news I can use.

I say I'm on the verge of a meltdown,
Got all kinds of blues—
Every time I seek to win,
I always seem to lose.

I'm on the verge of a meltdown!
Don't bother me, you hear?
I'm on the verge of a meltdown!
Child...you *need* to fear!

So please take ten steps back
And let me *cool* down.
I am begging for your silence.
Don't want to hurt you now!

'Cause I'm on the verge
Of a *melt*down,
So don't bring me bad news.
I'm on the verge of a meltdown.

Bring me some *good* news I can use!

Emotionless

I am *so* tired...
Emotionally drained,
Energy sucked out of me,
Drowning in a world of pain.

Can't stop the teardrops from falling,
Can't stop the pouring rain.

Today I surpassed that place
Called being "sick and tired."

Can't sink any lower—
Can't leap any higher.

Vicious

With fervent strength and swiftness,
I travel through time and space.
I embark upon the greatest of them
Representing *every* race.

I stampede upon the lowly
And all those in between
I have no prejudices as the world may seem.

I...*influence,*
Deceive,
And *destroy*...
The untrained,
The ignorant, and
The selfish.

I flow within the inner layers...of spiritual
Fibers, cells, and souls.

They...*carry* the seed,
    But it is I who *nurtures* it.

They...*birth* the seed,
    But it is I who *cradles* it.

They...*claim* the seed,
    But it is I who *influence* it.

So when they...*neglect* the seed,
    It is I who *possess* it.

Voices in Her Head

RamblingWeepingThumpingChatteringLaughingCreeping!
RamblingWeepingThumpingChatteringLaughingCreeping!
RamblingWeepingThumpingChatteringLaughingCreeping!

Too many old and unfiltered conversations
And multiple sounds are locked away and
Are boxed inside of her distorted mind.

All that has entered is now trapped inside.

She struggles psychologically to regain control
Of her mind...for that is where her sanity is
Secretly confined.

To release the pressure...she holds both hands
Over her ears and crawls into a corner on her
Worn-out marble floor...rocking back and
Forth like a fierce wind at shore.

Moaning and groaning, humming and mumming
To no particular beat...just attempting to quiet
Her soul momentarily.

But yet...
    In the background...
        She can still hear the multiple sounds...of

Children fighting,
Vehicles moving
    Hurriedly in the gusting wind;

Cats meowing,
Dogs barking, and
Birds *chirping,*
People yelling,
Babies crying,
Gunshots!
      And the sounds of falling bodies *dying*...

Doors squeaking,
Music playing,
Teachers teaching,
Preachers preaching,
Chalkboards squeaking,
Groans of lovemaking,
Shatters of glass breaking,
The sounds of heart-aching *music*!

Silence is the thing hoped for that may never
Be obtained inside that noisy mental wall
Called her brain.
Just...the

RamblingWeepingThumpingChatteringLaughingCreeping!
RamblingWeepingThumpingChatteringLaughingCreeping!
RamblingWeepingThumpingChatteringLaughingCreeping!

Dark Rage

Why do we rage?
Like hungry vultures,
Crime and brutality are the norm in this culture.

This barbaric hostility has no color,
Except it be dark rage.
It doesn't matter the locality, race, sex,
Economic status, or age.

Child molesters fester, and some only
Spend a few months in jail,
Though their victims are sentenced to
A lifetime of mental anguish and
Emotional hell.

Children being murdered in drive-bys,
Cut down like branches like they're on a
Battlefield.

Thugs loitering on the street corner,
Making heroin and crack deals.

Domestic violence is on the rise.
Both CEOs and the common Joes
Wear deceitful masks that grins and lies,
While in silence behind closed doors
Are the tortured screams of a woman's cry

Hatred and terror frequent our midst
From urban-hood to suburban-hood,
This barbaric hostility has no color,
Except it be dark rage.

People…*why* do we rage?

Just Wondering

I wonder what she's feeling
As she lies crying on her bed, *squealing*.
I wonder about the conversation
She's having in her head as she stares up
At the *ceiling*.

Curled up in a ball,
Knees folded to her chest,
While holding on to her pillow,
In a constant state of unrest,
As her infant child lay in his crib across
The room.

*Is she crying because she's happy or because
She pictures her doom?*

INFECTED! FULL BLOWN!
No cure to be known—*AIDS* radically thriving
In her body while tearing down her home.

The trace of every tearstain is ingrained in my
Mind as I wonder if she will also be alive
In the next month, the next year, or tomorrow.

For her, my heart beats with sorrow.

Wondering...how many more tomorrows
Will God allow her to borrow to see her newborn
Son take his first walk...his first run?

College-bound—though she wears an *uncertain*
Frown that periodically breaks her spirit down
And provokes aching screams without *sounds*.

She keeps reaching and reaching for her goals!
No AIDS—no disease will fade her future that
Remains *yet* untold!

So for the *moment*...her newborn son she
Beholds.

Yet, I'm still left wondering just as I'm sure
She's pondering: *How many more tomorrows
Will God allow her to borrow?*

How many more tomorrows will she be able
To borrow before the final day when her son
Will grieve in sorrow...*before her son will
Grieve in sorrow?*

No one knows, but still...I wonder.

White

Your massive ego would be laughable if it wasn't
So pathetic. So you've convinced yourself that you
Can handle me?

You say that you're even willing to bet it.

Do you *really* think you have a hold on me?
Just because you possess me doesn't mean that
I ain't free.

I roam in your dome like a king on his throne—
Making your eroded temple *my* home.

While you lay there *hazing*, I am *blazing*—
Feeding off of your membrane.
Inside yourself...not you, but I reign—
Taking you on a *high* to nowhere.

Got your mind so twisted,
You're in constant despair.

You think you got me because you bought me?
All you ever do is snort me!

When I get a hold of you, I make you bow down
And exalt me because *you'll* do anything to court me.

All I have to do is *exist*, and you'll sell your own soul
Just to get with some of this!

For me, you'll kill your own flesh and blood
Just to get another hit of your newfound love!

I reign in your brain,
Making you go insane without me.
You have no clout without me.

I reign over families, cities, and nations.
You see, there's no restriction to my habitation...
An explosion of *erosion*—an epidemic!

So you think you got a hold on me?
What a gimmick!

The Quiet Aching of Innocence

Little boy children
Should be left to bask
In the innocence of their youthful
Ignorance

With a mother and father to nurture
And care for them;

And not be punched in the chest
By his father, no less, and told to
"Man Up" when he cries;

Or be humiliated by his mother who
Calls him the name of a feline—the
Nickname given to that which lays in
Between her thighs;

Or be left by parents who place
More value on leaving him—
Rather than on staying—forgetting
The responsibility that comes with
Conceiving him.

Little boy children
Should be left to bask
In the innocence of their youthful
Ignorance…

Taught by teachers and coaches

Who inspires, and challenges
Their minds, and creativity;

And not be preyed upon and
Primed to become their next victim
Of Pedophilia;

Or not have their intelligence insulted;
Or the light on their future dimmed
By those who've decided to know
What their future hold—better than
God—the master of the universe who
Endowed us with the spirit to beat the odds.

Little boy children
Should be left to bask
In the innocence of their youthful
Ignorance...

And not be terrorized by the
Lingering stench of incest, bullying,
Or stray bullets that stalks their
Dreams—turning them into nightmares.

Little boy children should never know
Blues, but unfortunately,
Many of them do.

Yet, they are taught to be silent
And not to share their emotions
At an early age.

NOT ANOTHER TEAR: MOVING FROM PAIN TO PURPOSE

So their pain often festers and
Turns into quiet rage
That sometimes becomes uncaged.

Contrary to popular belief,
Little boy children, hurt too.
And when they become a man,
They still bear the scars of their
Youth.

But we have turned a blind eye.
We neither see, nor hear their
Cries.

But just because we are
Accustomed to being
Thoughtlessly unaware,
It doesn't mean that their
Pain isn't there.

Deep inside them is a:
A hurt,
A longing,
And a certain kind of
Loneliness

And behind the
Egos and masculinity is,
The quiet aching of innocence.

#TheQuietAchingOfInnocence
#MenHurtToo

Dismissed

I wanted to be dismissed—dismissed from class
Although the school bell hadn't officially rung
And although my enrollment hadn't long begun.

Waking up for me was a daily disappointment!
No daily remedy of prescribed miracle ointment
To soothe my cares away or to keep my pain
At bay.

A *complete* misery!
A total waste of my time.
Many mornings I woke up to a world
That felt less and less like mine.

Lying in bed with the covers
Draped over my head—staring like a
Mouse in a maze—in a gaze…
Have you ever had those kinds of days?

Not wanting to arise to participate
In the classroom madness of life
Because the pain cuts deep like a knife!

Drowning—immersing deep in my own
Despair—I couldn't imagine in this world
That someone actually cared.
…I cared.

Sometimes I Wonder

Sometimes I sit back and wonder,
What has caused your pain—
the pain that looms at the bottom
of the one hundred percent proof
you often consume in great proportion?

When you take that last drop as it
drips onto your lips and tongue—as you
sip until you trip and grow numb—do
you taste the total sum of the agony of your
pain?

Sometimes I sit back and wonder,
Why are you so hateful and disregarding?
Why haven't you ever been willing to try
to address the monsters that are clearly
inside?

You unsuccessfully try to hide
them in the crack pipes you smoke through and
in the booze that consumes you, and
in a temper that flares that you resort to…
when you don't get your way.

It is my prayer that one day you won't
need your liquid or powdered crutches.
For, the things you cling to are the things that
are destroying you, and that keeps you crippled.

This makes them your masters
and you, the enslaved.

Don't you think it's time for you
to be brave by getting the help
you need?

The decision is yours:
Remain Captive, or Freed.

For, you are the *true* master
of your fate.

On the Shoulders We Stand Upon

Today

Today we celebrate our history.
Our fight for freedom and justice is no great mystery.

Come on now...you've heard the story!

Many of our ancestors toiled, bled, and died, and
Were criticized, ostracized and dehumanized
All because of their race.

What a disgrace!

We were all made by the same mind.
Intertwined together by the *molding* and *holding*,
Shaping and *making* of a holy God, who lets us know
That we were *all* made in his image.

So *every* race is of the same face!

So what is this I hear?
Prejudice, racism, and hatred still reign!
What do any of us hope to gain?

Deceiving ourselves by believing that one race is
Superior, and anything other than is inferior.
We must suffer from delirium!

'Cause other than *skin tone*, *tresses*, and *culture*
We're not that different from one another.

When you cry—when we cry,
Our tears are clear the same!
When you laugh—when we laugh,
Our faces glow like the golden sun, which is set above…
And, like a tan, leaves an imprint in the form of laugh
Lines that makes its presence known.

When you die—when we die—we are all buried
And are turned to dust from whence we came.
When you succeed—when we succeed,
We are *engulfed* with excitement and cheer.

When you bleed—when we bleed,
It is colored like *scarlet, roses,* or *fear.*

When you hate—when we hate,
We *all* lose the essence of our humanity
That causes us to be diseased with generations
Upon generations of passed-down insanity.

We become a society bankrupted,
Not of money but of soul and logic,
Respect and love for *all* humankind…
Tainted of the mind!

Not fully aware…of the immaculate, miraculous,
Spiritually motivated, God-equipped, and cultivated…
The one who said, *"Let there be…"*

Human and Spiritual conception…
Called into purpose by a holy God
To create what we now call *humanity.*

NOT ANOTHER TEAR: MOVING FROM PAIN TO PURPOSE

So again...I ask the question: What is this I hear?
Prejudice, racism, and hatred still reign?
What do any of us hope to gain?

We are all made by the same mind,
Intertwined together by the *molding* and *holding*—
Shaping and *making* of a holy God who lets you
And I know that we were *all* made in *his* image.

So *every* race is of the *same* face!

Flame

We carry the torch
In our walk—branded
To make incredible strides,
We carry the torch gracefully
Between the linings of our thighs.

We are women and men of destiny,
Moving beyond our pasts, for we
Know that through our experiences,
Troubles aren't meant to last.

And that's why we're not hidden
And refuse to be masked.
Our pasts have no control of us
Except when we give it the task.

So make up your minds
That you will be purpose defined,
No longer dwelling on the past,
Keeping your souls confined.

The world is waiting for your gifts,
So reach for the stars, and
I don't care where you came from,
Because your past is *not* who you are!

So walk boldly into your bright futures,
Beautiful children of God.
Affirm to yourself daily

NOT ANOTHER TEAR: MOVING FROM PAIN TO PURPOSE

That you will beat the odds.
So refuse to think low.
Set and aim your arrow high,
And remember that failure is only
For those who simply refuse to try.

This is just the beginning—
The place where we *all* must start
So whatever you must do in the meantime,
Do it! Be encouraged, and don't lose heart.

Instead, let your passion for *purpose*, *hope*,
Success, and *love* blaze like fire—flow deep
Like blood in your veins.

And remember that, in spite of the obstacles,
There will be change!

Yes, we all can make it
Because *together*, we carry the FLAME!

On the Shoulders We Stand Upon

The road to greatness is paved with pain, unfairness, trials, and even failures. Therefore, we mustn't be afraid to forge ahead in the face of any of them. Our remarkable history as a people teaches us that. To fail and get up again is within our heritage. In doing so, we'll find ourselves in the company of the greats.

Langston Hughes, Les Brown, Dr. Maya Angelou, Bayard Rustin, Martin Luther King Jr., Booker T. Washington, Alex Haley, Dr. Carter G. Woodson, Derek Walcott, Wanda M. Austin, Benjamin Banneker, George Alcorn, Otis Boykin, Marian Croak, George Washington Carver, Cicely Tyson, James Earl Jones, James Edward West, Augusta Savage, Alice Coachman, Alice Walker, Terry McMillian, Althea Gibson, Tina Turner, Diane Carroll, Aretha Franklin, Cicely Tyson, Sojourner Truth, Mamie Lue Hamer, Gladys Knight, Redd Foxx, Pattie Labelle, Shirley Chisholm, Prince, Amelia Boynton, Hattie McDaniel, Madam C. J. Walker, Clara Brown, Marcus Garvey, Oprah Winfrey, Michael Jackson, Former First Lady Michelle Obama and President Barack Obama…and the list goes on and on.

To never give life a fighting chance—to make your own incredible mark and impact in this world—is to be in the company of the idle. To refuse to live out your calling is to crack the backs and wound the shoulders of our ancestors…the same shoulders that carried their immeasurable pain and their immeasurable promise. *We are their promise!*

They were the essence of profound and stubborn strength that gave life to *our* possibilities. We should stand upon these shoulders gloriously...to build the kind of life that many of them were denied. Our people suffered the unspeakable.

For every drop of their blood spilled as a result of inhumane beatings and the hangman's noose, *live a life of love and nonviolence!*

For their rotting flesh that hung from the trees, *live a life of humanity and peace!*

For every drop of sweat that poured like water from their beaten brow beneath the unrelenting and scorching sun, *live passionately in the pursuit of your dreams!*

For every underground railway that bears the historic footprints of those who ran for their freedom—*with an urgency of now—chase after your divine destiny, and don't stop running until you achieve what is rightfully yours!*

For every tear cried because of a lifetime of terror, suffering, and uncertainty, our people faced each day, *live life with intent, wonder, hope, faith, and perseverance!*

For their children who were taken and sold like cattle to the highest bidder, *embrace and cherish your children, and teach them that their value is priceless and can never be rented or bought!*

For their humanity that was stripped from them, *hold your head up unashamed, with a boldness of certainty that your equality can never be downgraded to inferiority!*

For their brutal rapes and mass violations they endured, *stand up against predators and seek justice*!

For being denied their right to vote, *show up to the polls, and cast your vote—for your vote is not a reflection of the voice of one but the voices of many—representing all of the shoulders we stand upon who fought for us to have this right*!

For being denied their right to drink from the same water fountain as whites, to sit in the same classroom as whites, to be given the same opportunities as whites, or to sit on the front of the bus as whites, *keep drinking from where you damn well please, sit not only in front of the bus but also in front of the class, and achieve excellence in your endeavor to be educated.*

For every vile act against them *pay homage to them by being the best version of yourself as humanly possible, seizing every opportunity, breaking down every barrier, and by doing your absolute best to live each day with intent, and with a strong sense of pride and purpose. For we owe this to them and to ourselves*!

For we are not inferior! We are equal; therefore, we must continue to stand up against inequality—and not just for brown people—but for *all* people. We must think and speak unity.

God gave breath, power, and purpose to each of us, across every color dimension, and across every nation! We are *a part of an equation* called the *Human Race,* and are not the total sum.

Yes, alone, we are brilliant, tenacious, resilient, and beautiful masterpieces birthed out of a divine mind.

Yes, alone we are powerful! However, together, we're powerful to *unknown* dimensions. For what we are capable of together far exceeds what we are capable of as one.

Our future is ever-unfolding—our possibilities are yet unknown! Our time of adding to the richness of our fabric as unrelenting, unstoppable, creative, spiritual, forgiving, diverse, gifted, loving, agents-of-change, and way-making geniuses is now!

Therefore, we must forgive the past and not judge an entire race of people because of the poison of racism and hatred of those within that race.

We must be cautious not to become what we hate, even in a society that still carries the lingering stench of the old and new-age "isms," and prejudices that perpetuate the ugliness of violence, hatred, self-hatred, injustice, and racism!

For the shoulders we stand upon are massive and strong.

It is our responsibility as well as our right, to exemplify the strength of our foundation and the love that springs forth from it.

Together we stand! Together we conquer!

Divided...we crumble!

Carrying to Term

Regardless of the difficulty
and uncertainty of it all,
I shall carry to term, the
blessings granted.

When I can no longer
carry them inside of me—when
my walls open up from the
pressure—on the cusp of
revealing themselves, I shall
press down, exhale and push
forth those I carry until
they crown and spring forth.

When they finally reveal
themselves—I shall greet them
joyfully.

As they grow, I shall continue
nurturing them with gratitude,
love, and guidance.

The challenge, fear, and pain
that accompany the dreams I
carry, does not diminish the hope,
value, and the agonizing need, to
carry them to term.

#ImpregnatedWithPurpose
#CarryingToTerm

Dear God,

As I reflect back upon my life and my life experiences, I can clearly see your loving hands, and your grace, maneuvering… making ways for me. Even when I rejected you, you never left me. I would not have made it out of my darkest hours had you not been there.

I would hate to think what my life would have turned out to be had you turned away from me, as I had done you. Out of all the shoulders I stand upon, it has been the strength of yours that has carried me the farthest and lifted me up the longest.

You have sustained me in every facet of my life—in every struggle, every triumph, every lesson, and every joy. Had you not had your hand on my life, what I see now as traumas and failures that I've overcome, could have easily been tragedies that consumed me.

You were the whisper in the dark—the dream of me falling—commanding me to pick myself up again and again, and refuse to be defeated.

You were the cool breeze that ran across my chest in the middle of the night when my heart was hurting.

You were the ease to my troubled and trapped mind—the light that lit my path when all surrounding me was darkness. You were the stranger who fed me when I was hungry— and the grace that covered me from harm when I was yet ignorant of you, or the dangers that my saturated eyes could not see.

You were the resilience and the fire inside of me that refused to allow me to give up in college as I had done in high school.

You were the strength that I stood on, and up against, when life had weakened me.

I wanted a future that exemplified the very reason I showed up here on this planet; the very reason my conception had to be; the very reason I had to take the path I did; and the very reason I was compelled to purchase a one-way Greyhound bus ticket at seventeen years old, alone, ignorant, desperate, and depleted, with only five dollars in my pocket, some mustard-seed faith, and a sparkle of hope—moving more than eight hundred miles away from everything and from every one I had ever known, or ever loved.

Now, here I am standing, and not because I am so strong but because your grace is sufficient. For whatever reason, you have walked alongside me—have carried me even—even when I resented you. I am forever grateful that in you, I have found relentless, remarkable, and unconditional love.

Love

Love...
There's nothing like it!

Sultry.
      Exotic!
           Soothing.
Hypnotic!

Unconditional and Everlasting—
    It can be yours for the asking!

Beautiful and Unique—
Makes every void complete.

Sensitive and Kind—
Pure, Real, and Genuine!

Exhilarating and Grand.
    How much of this love do you think you can stand?

Wholesome and Meek,
Sensational and Tender,
    To it, will your soul surrender?

Alpha and Omega,
The Beginning and the End,
    An everlasting friend...JEHOVAH GOD!

    Now that's Love!

The Satisfaction of Labor

There is nothing like
A dream that springs forth—
After laboring intensively,
To give birth to it.

When Agony Becomes Certain

There is a certain agony
That comes with pushing—that
Propels us to want to give up—
Followed by a burst of strong
Will that propels us even more,
To keep pushing.

You've got to keep pushing!
Never give up.

#WhenAgonyBecomesCertain
#KeepPushing!
#NeverGiveUp!

Healing Must Be Demanded

Some people nurse wounds of the past,
keeping their horrific experiences alive
in the forefront of their minds—
replaying the tragic scenes of yesterday
by giving them breath and power.

Though your past experiences were real,
the past is now impotent—void of power,
so why continue giving life to a series of events
that are deserving of death?

Focus on healing instead of hurt,
forgiveness instead of hate,
peace instead of misery,
faith instead of fear,
and success instead of failure.

Focus on the here and now!

And with life's ever-unfolding and
unlimited opportunities—
and with your extraordinary
potential—focus on a future, *unmatched,
untouched, and untampered with* by any past
that you may have had to crawl out of.

I Cry No More

I Cry No More

I cried for the little girl who
Lived on the inside of me,
    The little girl who had a rather *bleak* destiny...
And for the woman who was waiting to be free...
The woman *long* dead inside of me.

I cried for all the times I spent
In the park *alone* in early morning...late at night,
    With *no* place to call home...
And for all the times that
I was hungry and scared, barefoot and wet,
    Wishing for death!

I cried for *every* moment
I slept with *boy*friends as a teen
Not because I loved them but because I had no other
Means...no means of *getting* love...of *being* loved
By another, with a simple hug or
A common touch...one that would validate
    Who I am...what I am!
One that would bring me home inside myself
And say...*I love you.*

I cried for my soul,
The young soul that had grown old and weary,
    Cold and *dreary* because neither it nor she
    Belonged.
Cried for the little girl and for the grown woman
    Trapped in *every* unhappy song.

Cried for my soul!
For it was *scarred* and *bruised* with mountains of
Heartache, pain, and despair...
      Cried because no one seemed to care!
I cried for the little girl
Who was held down to be *violated* and *raped*!
      Cried mountains and rivers, valleys and streams.
Cried blood, hatred, sorrow, and tears!
Oh, how I cried for crying through the years!

I cried for the *loss* of my grandmother all those years
Before and how I missed belonging to someone...
      Someone whom I adore.
Cried for the *many* times my own mother *tore* me down
With words like, *I wish you were never born*!
Despite the fact she didn't raise me...
      In my heart I mourned.

I cried for the loss of my virginity at fourteen-years-old
Because I was too intoxicated to tell the
Nineteen-year-old "no."

I cried because at twenty-five I *didn't* know myself
And because I was depleted—had no more soul left.
Cried because others *failed* to get to know *my* pain.
For they only saw the outside of me and
      Not my own disdain!
Cried for *my* daughter for being born to a *teenage* mother
Who couldn't *even* perceive her own worth—
      A woman-child who had yet to establish her own
Worth.

NOT ANOTHER TEAR: MOVING FROM PAIN TO PURPOSE

I cried in 1998 when I *heard* the shackles removed...
Dropping from my soul,
When God told me through his Word
I am worth far more than gold!
Cried when he commissioned me not to be
What others said I was but what he said I *am*...
    I am more than a conqueror!

I cried when he whispered,
You've been given life not to suffer
    But to enjoy for all it's worth.
That day was the true day of my God-given birth.
Cried because God said that I am *his* temple
And to him *I* belong.
Never ever again shall my soul be
    The *essence* of some unhappy song.

I cried, and I cried.
For it was on that day my soul was *revived*,
And the sad little girl in me quietly waved good-bye,
    And the woman long dead inside of me *finally*
    Came alive!

Yesterday I cried until my body ached.
Cried *deep*, *long*, and *hard*!
In secret places I cried!
In small and wide-open spaces, I cried!
In the rooms I managed to dwell in for one night
Or two, I cried!
Oh, how I cried bitter cries!

Cried hilltops and oceans!

Cried angry regrets and bitter memories!
Cried for myself and for others like me!
I cried because I was *sick* and *tired* of crying!

And when the *crying* was over...
My soul began to crack a smile, laugh, dance,
And shout for joy!

For I could cry no more!

You see, I cried my way out of *bondage*!
Cried my way out of *shame*!
Cried my way out of *insanity*!
Cried my way out of disdain!
Cried my way out of the crying game!

And then I *prayed* my way to freedom.
And I *prayed* my way to peace.
Today *I am* set free...free inside of me.

And so today...*I cry no more!*

When You Speak My Name
(An Open Letter: My Response to Sexism and Racism in America)

When you speak my name with vain utterances in your failed attempts to try and capture me in the web of your decaying tongue, your words echo like useless chatter. Your lying mouth is like a dog without teeth—you have no bite. Your mere words become noise to my ears, like a bad song playing on the radio that I *turn* off.

When you speak my name and say that I am weak because I am a woman, remember, it is the strength of my womb that enables me to give birth to nations and that enabled your mother—also a woman—to give birth to you. And for that, her womb did not become your tomb...your final resting place at your conception. It was her strength that kept you alive, nurtured you, and pushed you out into your destiny—from one dimension... and into the one you now find yourself in. And there will come a day—at an appointed time—when *God will speak your name as well as mine*—pushing us from this dimension and into the next.

When you speak my name with condescending overtones and racist slurs or treat me unjustly, in vile attempts to define me, to cage me, or to diminish my essence, you *shrink* your own. I *cannot* be reduced! I am flesh! I am blood! I am spirit! I am love! I am God's masterpiece! Designed out of the omnipotent, all-wise, creative, loving, genius, and divined mind of supreme brilliance—*I was chosen!*

When you speak my name, why encage yourself with hatred toward me? *I'm not your enemy!* I am your sister—our spiritual DNA makes it so! My apologies—if this upsets you or shatters your delusion of grandeur—*but even you must realize that an illusion isn't real.* An illusion is just that...an illusion—an impotent imposter appearing real to the *insecure, hateful, and vain* imagination of small and tainted minds. **You were never meant to be small...and nor was I!**

Like me, your beauty and significance is also God's Masterpiece, so why do you detest me? That isn't a question I wish to know the answer to, because quite frankly, your answer really doesn't matter because your hatred has *no* validity!

Had I sought to disrupt *your* destiny or raped your daughters, wives, mothers, sisters, brothers, and...sons, had I sold *your* children into slavery or slaughtered generations of *your* people—hanging them like ornaments on a tree to rot, as I cheered proudly at this form of sickening brutality, had I murdered their promises and their possibilities, as well as their dreams.

Had I dehumanized them to make *myself* feel grand as I filled *my* pockets with greed that *they* slaved for under inhumane conditions—*it was all inhumane;* had I stolen from you...*then* I would understand. I would understand your contempt toward me, but I did *nothing* to you! No...that was actually *your* people who did that to mine. Yet I do not hold you *personally* responsible because of your shared skin tone and tresses. This is in spite of the trail of my ancestors' blood that's colored like crimson and pours like liquid gold from your ancestors' hands...*and that now stains your own.*

Ravaged with greed and hatred, love did not reside in *their* hearts. *They tore my people's world apart!* And the ripping of those tares...in many of us we still bare...because the magnitude of that kind of depravity, simply *can't just heal* with the passing of time—especially when you remind us so well of your hatred spell...lest we ever forget your hate. *We shall never forget*...but nor shall we surrender ourselves to it. Now you stand guilty of the same? Though your acts of hatred differ to some degree—it is hatred just the same. Nevertheless, it would be *silly* of me to judge an entire race of people because of the vile acts of some within *that* race, including yours...or even my own. So, I'm asking for you to ponder: *Why do you hate me so... when you speak my name?*

When you speak my name, why must you do so in vain and with poisonous tongues? *It was my people that were hung!* Though you spread your venom...I shall not drink your poison! For I know *who* I am, *why* I am, and *whose* I am. For every drop of hatred you ingest—*it is you,* and not I, who become less—as you slowly kill off the essence of your own humanity and that of your offspring. I shall not do the same! *I choose love. I will never dance to the beat of your suffering, bare cast down eyes upon you with glee, or turn a blind eye to any wrong that befalls you because I value your essence, your reason for being, and your humanity. For, we are all God's children.*

So when you speak my name, why do you not think it is foolish and strange to treat what God has created with such contempt because of the color of my skin...the skin that *He* put me in? Even the rainbow—baring its own uniqueness and beauty—bears not one color that is *inferior or superior* to the other. *They are merely...different, but each...beautiful just the same.* We are mere strokes of paint off the tip of a paintbrush on a canvas that has no end. So then please tell me how dare you muster up the audacity to offend…by telling an infinite and all-wise creator that what *HE* created is flawed and inferior, while yet deeming yourself the race that is superior *rather* than EQUAL?

This would be laughable if it wasn't so sad. For, on our *best* day, we can't out-do God in any capacity, and yet you have this extraordinary audacity to speak in this vein? You do not qualify to create the definition of me or to determine the value of *me*. Yet, you persist! You call my beauty, ugly; my brown, inferior; my value worthless; and my mind, inept—*when you speak my name*.

When you speak my name—do so…*with love* because I am love. And when I speak *your* name, *I* shall do the same. For I do not wish to become what I hate. Should you choose to do otherwise—know that—like the tide in the ocean and like Angelou's poetry, *I'll rise!* Like the sun and like air, I will still be here. And I'll rise, and I'll also shine! *You cannot hold me down!*

When you speak my name and seek to employ ways to try to disrupt *my* destiny with all of your "isms"—killing me off slowly—ten million more like me shall rise. For love conquers hate, and *destiny* conquers your damnation. **THIS IS GOD'S NATION and WE ARE ALL HIS CREATION! SO HUMBLE YOURSELF!**

When you speak my names…*remember* to whom you speak about. *I am your sister! I'm your sister.*

You were conceived like me.
You conceive like me.

NOT ANOTHER TEAR: MOVING FROM PAIN TO PURPOSE

You were born like me.
You breathe like me.
You cry like me.
You bleed like me.
You smile like me.
You get down like me.
You frown like me.
You fly like me.
You're fly like me.

You're third-dimension bound like me.
So, while you're living, you ought to give agape love,
*A try like me...*before you *die* like me...
Because you're like me, so like me. I love you...

...When I speak your name.

Hometown Girl: Aiken, South Carolina

To gaze at your *dazzling* stars in the serenity of midnight
As they glisten without sound in beautiful formation.

To play outside with my cousins and all of my kin,
Laughing and *running* and *jumping* and *screaming*...acting
Wild and *crazy*!

To sit on the edge of the front porch, swinging my legs
Back and forth—*bare feet*—all on a hot summer
Afternoon while guzzling down red Kool-Aid and just
Being *lazy*.

To skip through the halls while gliding my *not-so-clean*
Fingers up and down the walls of Aiken Elementary.

To sit in the classroom at Scofield Middle, listening as
Lessons were revealed, or to gaze outside the windows
Inattentively—*hey, I'm just keeping it real.*

Because...

To smile again, to be a child again, just for a moment...
'Cause I'm a hometown girl!

To go back and erase all the wrong I did as a kid and to
Perhaps correct some of my many regrets.

To stroll down Kershaw, Horry, Union, Fairfield, and Sumter
Streets in the blistering summer heat.

NOT ANOTHER TEAR: MOVING FROM PAIN TO PURPOSE

To sit in the quaint living room of Ms. Doretha Brown,
My history school teacher, as she personified the lesson
She aspired to teach me. Without ever making a sound—
She reached me.

To stand in the doorway, watching and listening to every
Word my grandmother said—to watch her laugh and even
Yell or to hear some of the stories she'd tell.

I really do miss her...I tell ya.

To smile again, to be a child again, just for a moment...
'Cause I'm a hometown girl

To kiss John one last time even though I knew he was a jerk,
But sometimes you love "love" even when love hurts but love
Ain't supposed to hurt.

To hear the records play at the Co-Co Cabana—shaking it on
The dance floor—*I really don't miss that anymore.*
Well...maybe every *now* and *then*.

To hear my great-grandmother hum and moan with intensity
Until water swelled up in her eyes as she cut up chicken and
Collard greens while baking sweet potato pies—though her
Songs were songs of mystery—somehow they spoke to the
Soul in me!

Oh...to smile again, to be a child again, just for a moment
'Cause I'm a hometown girl!

To lie down beside my grandmother in bed when no
One's around—feeling the love I felt without her ever
Making a sound.

To watch Aunt Pauline over on Horry Street, cooking
Squash in bacon grease as the scent perfumed the air—
Yeah...periodically, my mind goes there.

To be walked to school by my uncle Melvin faithfully
Each day—as I skipped along singing my song, he'd walk
Me all the way.

I tell ya...
I wish I could smile again, be a child again, just for a
Moment, 'cause I'm a hometown girl.

At my first sight, you held me in your breath, Aiken, and
Sometimes you were breath taken! And I inhaled
You...ooh aah—ooh aah.

You caressed my skin—you *still* hold my kin!
You were my oxygen—my *everything* back then!

Aiken...how I still *ache* for you sometimes...*sometimes*
I said, Aiken! How I still *ache* for you sometimes...
Sometimes,

'Cause...

To smile again, to be a child again, just for a moment...
'Cause I'm a hometown girl.

I said to smile again, to be a child again...just for a moment

I said to smile again,
To be a child again.
I said to smile again,
To be a child again.

I said to smile again, to be a child again...just for a moment
'Cause I'm a hometown girl!

Simply Beautiful

You...
Oh, beautiful one, are a masterpiece,
brilliantly and strategically designed
by the world's *greatest* artist.

More priceless than Van Gogh and all
others combined. Artistry such as this,
the world will never create or
adequately define.

For *your* work of art was created by
supernatural design.

Amateurs call you flawed, but to him—
your creator—you are an *astonishing* and
flawless piece of art.

So love your *blackness* and what *your*
beauty holds—love *whatever* your color
and shape is.

For diamonds aren't just set in gold!

When God created you—yes, child,
he "broke the mold" because you are
simply beautiful.

Oh, Bully, Please!

So you think...
If you call me nasty names to try and put me down,
I'll get bent out of shape and turn this *gorgeous* smile
Into an *ugly* frown?

Sorry to disappoint you...
But *child*...that ain't even what's going down.

I'm going to hold my head up high—high toward the sky.
You can yell obscenities, but you'll *never* make me cry!

So, spend your life and all your energy trying to break
My spirit, but these precious ears ain't even trying to
Hear it—so fear it!

Cause I've got the power to compose myself—
For with dignity and grace I stand,
In the midst of your ghetto drama
My power still rests firmly in the clutches of
These hands.

You say you want to fight me
Because you've *decided* not to like me.
You don't even know me—so show me—
The logic in your animalistic behavior.
Oh, bully please!

You need a *savior*.

Still Standing

As I walked with my head bowed low,
I heard the snickering sounds of laughter
And harsh name-calling everywhere I'd go.

At the grocery store, and the laundromat.
At school, and in the streets, too.

Sometimes I sit back and wonder,
Whatever became of you?

Are you still standing idle,
Wasting your time—trying desperately
To build up your own poor self-esteem—
By tearing down somebody's like mine?

Does your character still reek of ugliness?
For cruelty has no beauty—
Meanness of spirit toward me
Was your constant and primary duty.

I am glad that I was able to help diverge
Your attention away from *your* own reality.
Perhaps you needed me
More than you'd like to believe.

For eight long years…
From elementary to middle school,
You tormented me with your words
And beat me down with your sudden blows,

NOT ANOTHER TEAR: MOVING FROM PAIN TO PURPOSE

Attempted to break my spirit,
And keep it depressed and low.

Do you remember how you
Bullied me with your groupies
Because I walked alone?

You didn't look my way, though,
When left standing on your own.
Were you afraid of me then?

No groupies to hold me down
Or to instigate your first blow
Just you and me standing...
Head-to-head and toe-to-toe.

I remember when I approached you
Alone on that warm and sunny day,
Fuming from my nostrils—I was the
Predator, and you were the prey.

Your voice crumpled with emotions
When I threatened to make you pay.

Did you ever tell your groupies
Why you *suddenly* left me alone?
Did you tell them that you were *reduced*
To nothing when left standing on
Your own?

Yet...I still remained strong although
I walked alone!

Shine

In anguish and fear,
I sit and wonder
If I'm forever stuck here,
Living beneath my calling
Like a broken-down car, I've been stalling
Ain't going nowhere—
Sitting on side of the road.

But I want more!

This is my time to shine!
So no more sitting on the curbside,
Watching life pass me by—
Hoping and wishing for better days—
Tears falling as I pray:

Lord, help me to believe
In my divine purpose and destiny.
There has to be more to life than this.
Bursting with passion, caged by fear.
Oh, I know I don't belong here.
I want more!

While telling myself that it's too late—
A contradiction of *fear* and *faith*—
Aborted dreams and broken wings!
Oh, I need you, and I want more!

This is my time to shine!

Sleep Sweetly

Never knew how much I needed you
Never knew how much you cared
Until I looked around and found that
You were no longer there.

Never thought that you were leaving
Always assumed you'd be
Riding the waves of life, and watching
Me reach maturity.

Yesterday...
You were standing here—
Strong and tall in stature.
Then suddenly, you were gone
Without a trace, and without a
Goodbye.

Time was the culprit that
Took your breath away
And now I sit here crying
With nothing left to say,

Except that I am hurting
Badly inside. You were the
Only one who loved me until
The day you died.

Inside my soul cries!

I don't understand why this had to be.
For years I've wondered, and for
Years I've grieved.

Although I'll *never* release you from
My heart, I've long decided to
Create a brand-new start by letting
You go, and letting God
Heal my heart.

So, sleep *sweetly*
For, you were my mother
Right from the very start.

You were my mother, and
I love you with my *whole* heart.

For you are my mother…
I love you…but now I must say…
Goodbye.

So, sleep…sweetly.

Inside

Inside...
I feel like a *rosebud*,
Beautifully unfolding—becoming
What destiny has called me to be!

Inside...
I feel like a *saxophone*,
Playing sweet, resounding, and
Sensual melodies of heart songs.

Inside...
I feel like an *ocean*,
Strong, fierce, and *purifying*
The essence of life!

Inside...
I feel like a *cool breeze*,
Caressing the earth's atmosphere and
Everything in it, as I travel through
Time and space.

Inside...
I feel like *living*!
Like living inside...I feel.
Inside...I feel *'real'* good.

Swim Lessons

I've had enough heartache
And I've made my own share
Of mistakes.

In the softness of midnight—
In the Springtime—
I can still hear faintly
The shattering...
When the heart breaks.

I've cried enough tears to drown in,
But somehow, I learned to swim.

I've been given swim lessons baby
In the hardest way—through
Trial and error—but luckily
I've managed to stay...

Riding with the currents
That have pushed me along...
...And now I train for marathons.

Keep Dancing

You are like a beautiful song, composed by a *superior* mind.

Your melody is breathtaking and your tempo—
divine.

Every element of your song is perfection—
keep dancing.

A Special Tribute to Diane Patterson
"Give Pause"

Give Pause

When you awake in the newness of each morning with heaviness in your hearts—knowing that it is yet another space in time that you are without your *mother, sister, grandmother, confidant, or friend*, I encourage you—even in the midst of your tears...to take a deep breath, and give pause.

As you remember the 'Blue Sky Days' when you talked about nothing and *everything*, and when *all* was right in your world...give pause.

As you remember how tremendously blessed you were to have been strategically chosen by a sovereign God to share precious time and space, life lessons and games, thrills and ideas, thought-provoking, and *even* mindless conversations, laughter, and *yes*...oh yes...even tears, with an incredible Human Being in the embodiment of Ms. Diane Patterson... give pause.

As you remember her seemingly never-ending fussy ways, and her 'Southern Drawl' (although she is from the North)— *interesting I know*—and as you remember how her mouth would often fling open-wide with laughter, and you could see the gleam that was filled with life in her eyes...give pause.

As you remember the love and the advice she gave, and yes... even the numbers she *played*...from her *"Numbers' Bible,"* which was like a sport to her because she played it *strategically, passionately*, and *often*...give pause.

Give pause while you're yet *weeping*, give pause while you're yet *loving*, give pause while you're yet *hurting*, give pause while you're yet *longing,* and give pause while you're yet *remembering*!

Give pause as you remember that her *life story* and the profound imprint that's left in the hearts and minds of those whom she loved, and of those who returned that love, are far-far greater, than her *death* story.

As you remember the unfairness of the world and all that you have *lost,* while you yet mourn her loss…also remember… remember the *gain*, and give pause.

Celebrate Diane's life—*her life*—and rejoice that she came this way in her appointed time, and give thanks.
And oh yes…give pause.

May the memories and the love of Diane Patterson shine ever-so-brightly like a lamppost—de-magnifying the darkness of your days when your hurt seems insurmountable.

And may the loving arms of God, family, and friends, embrace you—giving you strength, courage, and comfort in this time of healing.

Word from the Author

Thank you for reading *Not Another Tear: Moving from Pain to Purpose*. My passion and desire has always been to empower, as well as, to entertain others. I hope *Not Another Tear...*has accomplished both.

Please check out the "Bonus Exercise" on the following few pages. If you have enjoyed any part of this project, please 'Share' with others. Additionally, if you would like to learn more product or service information, to sign up for our monthly newsletter, or to join our VIP Mailing List, please visit: www.HollingsWord.com.

Also, connect with me on Facebook or follow me on Twitter. I would love to connect. Be blessed! Be relentless! Be kind! Be encouraged...and always, *"Get Inspired!"*

Thank you for your support!

Bonus Exercise
How to move from your pain and into your purpose

Have you made a covenant with your pain, past mistakes, or with your disappointments because you've convinced yourself that they are far more powerful than you are?

Have you settled for the inferior because you don't believe that *better* is waiting for you, or that you *deserve* better?

If your answer is *yes* to either of these questions, then you've come to the right place, because I wholeheartedly understand. I spent half of my life making a covenant with my traumas after convincing myself that my life held little value.

However, somewhere along the way, I gathered up some mustard seed faith and the courage to believe that more was possible, even for me. I also realized that my life not only has value, but it also has purpose. Therefore, I decided to make a new covenant to resolve the past and to heal from it, and to live the life that God intended for me to live.

You too, have the capacity to chart new territories, gain new footing, to be emotionally healed, and to live the life that God intended for you. Your pain doesn't have to win, and guess what, it didn't. For if it had, you wouldn't be still standing. You would merely be someone else's memory because you'd be dead. Check your pulse. It's still beating, isn't it? You're still here! Your pain did not win!

On the following pages, I've listed the steps I previously took that enabled me to rise above the past. Additionally, I offer some advice under each of those steps. Hopefully, you'll find it helpful.

1. **Understand the real value of acknowledgement:**
   In my opinion, the first act of change is *knowing*— knowing that hurt exist, knowing why we hurt, how we got hurt, and who did the hurting. Be warned, in our quest to confront the truth, we may discover that we have been the culprit behind some of our own pain, and behind the pain of other people.

   Though this realization alone can be downright painful, it's important to acknowledge this truth as well. If we're unable or unwilling to take an honest assessment of where the hurt began, regardless of who did the hurting, it's impossible to navigate our way successfully through, and out of, the pain. This is the real value of acknowledgement.

2. **Give yourself permission to let the pain go:**
   Some of us carry around years of compounded traumas that becomes like rotten waste that eats us up on the inside. We repeatedly lament over our scars, but to no avail, do we find freedom from the tears we cry.

   This happens when we don't give ourselves the *permission to heal. Do you believe that you are worthy of the peace, joy, and freedom you will acquire when you grant yourself this permission?*

   We were never meant to carry the pain of our past into our

future, but we often do. It was costing me too much to keep holding on to my painful past. *What is holding onto yours, costing you?*

If you find that the cost is too high, (and any cost should be), then I urge you to make a deliberate and conscious decision to grant yourself the permission to heal. Spending one more year, month, week, or even another day locked inside of your hurt would be an injustice.

Declare to yourself now, *(despite how you may be feeling at this very moment)*, that you deserve to be free. Say it: I DESERVE TO BE FREE! Repeat this statement daily until you truly begin to believe it. And when you *finally* believe it, you'll begin to act in alignment with your newfound belief, and those action steps will become stepping stones to your healing.

3 **Cry baby cry:**
Crying is therapeutic and it's normal. Therefore, you should not equate crying with weakness. Sometimes a good long cry may be exactly what you need in order to *begin* the process of moving beyond your hurt. It's an act of cleansing and releasing. However, you must do more than simply shed tears. You must confront the issue that's producing them.

4 **Knowing when enough is enough:**
Now, contrary to advice number "3", when I said: "Crying is therapeutic," if you've been crying for years about the same hurt, honey dry your weeping eyes because you've had too much therapy! (I'm kidding) Seriously though, sometimes

we get stuck in this place of shedding tears, and never take the process any further. I want you to go further. Don't you deserve to?

Perhaps, now is the time to step into the next phase of your healing by addressing the deeper issue—with the attitude and will—of overcoming it. No one can put a timetable on your process of healing. I merely want to encourage you to lift your head out of the sand, and begin making your way through your pain.

5. **Getting help:**
Solicit the professional help and guidance from a qualified counselor or mentor, if necessary. While we can confront and overcome some traumas on our own, there are some that are too enormous to take on alone. Therefore, ask for help if you need to. And prayer helps too!

6. **Treat your troubles like pie:**
In haste, we often time try to take on too many things too soon, and all at the same time. This can leave us even more discouraged and depressed because the results aren't what we envisioned they would be. Don't mistake this kind of behavior for productivity; it is misleading.

When addressing your past, take on the attitude that you will treat your troubles like pie—slicing off one small piece at a time. In other words, don't try to deal with the ten negative things that happened to you, or *all* of the mistakes you've made, all at once. Instead, address one of them, and be deliberate about not moving on to the next traumatic experience until you have successfully tackled the one. Repeat this process until your emotional plate becomes empty of all of the pain associated with the traumas, or your past mistakes.

7   **Don't play the *blame* game:**
Your emotional healing is too important for you to be stuck on *who is to blame*. Those at fault may not care one way or the other about your emotional scars, or how you actually got them. Therefore, while you should acknowledge the source, take up no residence in blaming.

Your healing is all that matters, and that, can never be contingent upon the responses you get from those who hurt you. Besides, you can't change the past but you can certainly prevent the past from altering your future. You can also accept it, learn from it, forgive it…and move on.

8   **Forgive yourself and those who hurt you:**
Forgiving myself, and those who hurt me was one of the most dreadful and most difficult things I had to do. Nevertheless, it was critical that I forgave because forgiveness is in part, the key to overcoming.

Realize that forgiving others doesn't necessarily mean that you invite them to have a seat at your table. It simply means letting go of the hurt, which frees you to move forward. Some relationships are mendable while others are toxic. It's your decision regarding how you wish to move forward in these relationships. Hopefully, you'll choose wisely. You don't want to end something that has the potential to be beautiful once healed.

However, on the other hand, you don't want to hold on to a person who hurt you who is simply no good for you. Whatever you decide, remember, forgiveness equals real freedom, therefore, make it your quest.

9. **History takes direction from you:**
We aren't powerless victims of the past. We are overcomers! In reality, we possess the power but we need to take back ownership of it. The past is impotent and is nothing more than a fleeting memory that some of us have chosen to cling on to.

Speak to your history and give it new direction. Say to it: *You are not permitted to invade my present or my future. You do not get a say in how I live out the rest of my life, from this day forward. The power you had over me has now been deactivated!*

10. **Get rid of toxic connections:**
If you are serious about overcoming your pain and living in the space of your promise, be willing to assess your relationships with the *people, places, things and thoughts,* in your life. If you find that any of these are toxic for you and your possibilities, you must make a decision to let them go, so you can grow!

11. **Consume yourself:**
In tip number "5" I advised you to get help. To be perfectly honest, I didn't have an emotional support system in place when I took the challenge to confront my past. Therefore, I had to be both creative and willing, to confront this enormous issue, differently. Here are some of the things I did that worked for me:

- I consumed myself with books, motivational speeches, and sermons.

- I listened to—and read about people—who overcame even greater challenges than my own. Then, I adopted some of their advice and principles.

- I created and read positive affirmations, and repeated them daily. I posted them throughout my home to serve as reminders of my value, and the value of moving from a life of pain, to a life of joy and purpose.

12 Be willing to learn

Some of us are stuck in our conditions, not because we can't get out but because we refuse to learn. To make any progressive steps towards healing, we must be teachable. No one enters into this life knowing everything. We are all ignorant, in some capacity. Life is too massive for us to know everything in *five* lifetimes, let alone in one.

I used to be very stubborn before I decided to become teachable. However, one day I got tired of bumping my head, which led to me having to experience the same negative outcome over and over again. I decided that like my pain, my ignorance was getting too expensive! Therefore, I finally decided to adopt the posture of a student in order to learn the tools and knowledge necessary—to live a more well-rounded, trauma-free, and drama-free life. Always be willing to learn.

13 **Never give up on yourself:**
You are far too important—and possess too much potential—to be left wounded and stranded in the past. You may think to yourself: *How am I stranded in the past when I'm standing right here in the present?*

Please allow me to elaborate: You cannot be one hundred percent *present* while holding on to the *past*. Get yourself out of the threshold of history and drop those bags of rocks (traumas) you've been carrying. I know it's difficult. I know it's depressing. I know it's painful...but guess what else I know? I know that it will also be a tragedy if you decide to keep your pain and your depression. Regardless of how badly you feel, you must dig deep daily, and work on transforming your life. Never give up on yourself! You are far too important to be left stranded.

14 **Purpose is Divine:**
Last but certainly not least, there are some deeply rooted pain that only God can usher us out of. Time alone won't do it, and therapy alone won't do it. However, God is divine, and so is your purpose. He can set the path in motion to your complete healing, in a fraction of a second. Unless you skipped the front of this book, you've read, "At The Beginning of My Tears." There was something divine happening in that experience that exceeded my human capacity to fully understand.

I'm not dismissing the need for therapy; I'm simply saying, try everything positive that is available to you, including the Creator.

Best wishes to you on your journey—to move from pain to purpose. Please know that you are worth the trip!

Thanks again for your support!

~Hollingsworth

About the Author

Hollingsworth was a high school dropout when she boarded a Greyhound bus at age seventeen, with only five dollars in her pocket and a one-way ticket, alone and unknowingly pregnant. She left everything and everyone she knew in her hometown of Aiken, South Carolina in search for a better life. Eventually, she found that better life. She returned to school and now hold degrees in Business Management and Liberal Arts.

Hollingsworth is the author of the *"Not Another Tear"* book series, and the upcoming novel series, *"Victims of Circumstances."* She is also the creator of the speaking series, "The Dream Series: A Six Part Personal Empowerment Project," and "Pillow Talk" (Fun and intimate discussions and performances held in a group setting, using her spoken poetry to guide an evening of delightful conversations. Often coupled with music, wine and hors d' oeuvres to turn up the flavor of a sultry and poetic experience.) Further, Hollingsworth is a Recording Spoken Word Artist, and Empowerment Speaker who has performed on stage at the World Famous Apollo Theater, The Pennsylvania Convention Center, and at a number of other venues, delivering empowering performances and presentations.

Hollingsworth enjoys traveling, creative writing, laughter, and helping others to reach their highest potential. Hollingsworth also enjoys connecting with her readers, and can be contacted directly via email at: ask@HollingsWord.com. You can also *Friend* her on Facebook and *Follow* her on Twitter.

Book Description

"Not Another Tear: Moving from Pain to Purpose" is a collection of raw, thought-provoking, and powerful poems that unveils a well-balanced mixture of vulnerability and strength. Comprised of mostly poetry, it also has a few narratives that encompasses facets of the human experience.

Homelessness, rape, abandonment, abuse, fear, relationships, lust, love, loss, motherhood, depression, hatred, forgiveness, empowerment, and success are some of the many topics found in *"Not another Tear: Moving from Pain to Purpose."*

Additionally, Hollingsworth's collection of poetry wraps up with a bonus exercise: "How to move from your pain and into your purpose."

The bonus exercise was added to empower you with action steps that can serve as a springboard to help propel you to move from your pain, and into your purpose.

www.ingramcontent.com/pod-product-compliance
Lightning Source LLC
Chambersburg PA
CBHW070547010526
44118CB00012B/1257